songs

in the key of

solomon

John & Anita Renfroe

songs
in the key of
solomon

In the Word...
...and In the Mood

David C Cook®
transforming lives together

SONGS IN THE KEY OF SOLOMON
Published by David C. Cook
4050 Lee Vance View
Colorado Springs, CO 80918 U.S.A.

David C. Cook Distribution Canada
55 Woodslee Avenue, Paris, Ontario, Canada N3L 3E5

David C. Cook U.K., Kingsway Communications
Eastbourne, East Sussex BN23 6NT, England

David C. Cook and the graphic circle C logo
are registered trademarks of Cook Communications Ministries.

LCCN 2007933213
ISBN 978-1-4347-6775-2

© 2007 John and Anita Renfroe

The Team: Don Pape, Traci Depree, Theresa With,
Jack Campbell, and Susan Vannaman

Cover Design: The DesignWorks Group

Printed in the United States of America
Hardcover Edition 2007
International Paperback Edition 2008

1 2 3 4 5 6 7 8 9 10

122107

We dedicate this book to our parents,
Rev. J. C. and Vesta Renfroe, and John and Kay Pulliam.
These are the people who first showed us what it means to
love God and each other. Your legacies of love, devotion,
and commitment will impact generations of married lovers.
Thank you for loving each other so well.

contents

Interlude Two ... Total Communion

Encore

overture

W ho doesn't love a good love song? It doesn't matter if it's schmaltzy, cheesy, or sweet, or if it just perfectly reflects something you're feeling; love songs keep the romantic world spinning on its axis. They provide the sound track for your love life, from your first crush all the way to your fiftieth-anniversary waltz.

So our question to you is this: What song is playing between you and your lover?

Or maybe an easier question to answer is this: If you had to choose a ringtone for each other, what would it be?

- "(I Can't Get No) Satisfaction"
- "Strangers in the Night"
- "Theme from *Mission: Impossible*"
- "Let's Get It On"

A few years back, Patti Austin and James Ingram recorded the song "How Do You Keep the Music Playing?" for the movie *Best Friends,* and these are a few of the questions they asked:

How do you keep the music playing?

How do you make it last?

How do you keep the song from fading too fast?

How, indeed?

It's tough to keep the music playing in our marriage with all the other sounds vying for our attention and drowning out the rhythms that first drew us together. And it may have been so long since we heard the faint strains of love that they're now a misty memory or difficult to remember at all. If you're newly married, the music may seem like it's not quite coming together as smoothly as you had envisioned, or if you're a little further along in your marital journey, you may have quit listening to the music altogether.

Most married couples are connected more by mailing address and parental roles than by true intimacy. We're all dying to get back to the point of connection—the point of origin: a man and a woman, intimate before God. In a word, Eden. When you boil it all down ("it" being "everything") to the essentials, in the beginning there was God, a man, a woman, and nakedness. And it was really, really good. This nakedness was God's doing … at least until we messed the whole thing up. But in the pages of this book, we hope to draw you a little closer to Eden.

Some of you may be thinking, *How is the experience presented in this book going to be any different from the past five attempts we've made at trying to have some sort of devotional moments together?* You need to know that we totally get it. We understand why couples do exactly two of the devotionals in *any* book and then promptly decide to "lose" the book: mainly because the wife is the one driving the train, asking (OK, let's be honest … *nagging*) her husband to do the devo with her ("Please, please, please? Try it just this one week?"), trying to carve out the time, and trying to keep him interested. It usually ends up being one more thing she feels she has to spiritually shame him into

("You know, the Bible says you're *supposed* to be the spiritual leader …") and one more reason he winds up feeling like a spiritual loser. Let's tally that up: One feels like a nag, one feels like a loser. Not such a great outcome, right?

We know this because we're two committed believers who haven't found any guide or devotional for couples that lights our fire enough for us to stick with it. In fact, one of us is an ordained pastor, and the other is a Christian comedian, and we *still* can't get the devotional thing nailed down. We've often wondered why eternal truths that will bring us closer together, strengthen our marriage, and create something that will outlive us tend to make us hit the mental snooze button.

Wouldn't it be great if we found something that would wake us up to the privilege of being in God's Word together? Maybe another kind of devotional tool for couples that resulted in different feelings entirely. One in which the guy gets totally jazzed by the idea that he's going to have some "spiritual" fun with his woman. One in which the woman gets pretty enthused by the prospect that she's going to open another window into the soul of her man and find a place to connect with him on a spiritual and emotional level. We think you're holding that kind of devo in your hands. And if the first instruction in this book reads, "Run a nice bubble bath and wash a colander of grapes; then both of you climb in and read the next sentence," wouldn't you be eager to get started?

But before you start running the water, let us give you a

little heads-up on the format. We've created sixty encounters for you to enjoy with each other, including suggested settings—or "rhythms"—for every devo to mix it up a little. You know how it is when you do the same thing over and over and over and over again? It loses its freshness. Sometimes just getting into a different setting opens up your mind to other possibilities. But we don't intend for this to be a legalistic thing. If the suggestion is to lie in a sleeping bag in the backyard on a certain day, and it's raining cats and dogs outside, pick another devo or another location. Or use your own imagination to do something better than we thought up. We don't care *where* you do it, as long as you "Just Do It" (insert Nike commercial here).

Then we offer a passage of Scripture to reflect on (nothing too lengthy because we think you can do inductive, cross-referenced, highlighter-driven Bible studies individually). We've called this section "Listen to the Music." Next we talk a little about "What We Hear" when we listen to the music. After that we ask you, "What Do You Hear?" and give you a few conversation starters so that you'll have a chance to talk about what you heard in the Scripture reading. We also offer an "Extended Play" suggestion that may add another level of fun or challenge to your encounter. We have great expectations of taking the biblical principle of "naked and … not ashamed" (Gen. 2:25 NASB) to the next level.

We believe another way to pronounce the word *intimacy*

is "into me see" because we all desire to be fully known and loved by the person we've committed ourselves to in marriage. In years past Christendom had an unwritten rule that there was to be spiritual intimacy between a person and God, emotional intimacy with (an understanding of) another person, and physical intimacy between a man and woman, and that these tributaries would only occasionally, perhaps accidentally, converge. But these man-made constructs prevent us from seeing all these areas of intimacy as potential spiritual connections that bring us closer to each other and, thereby, closer to God. Both marriage partners want spiritual intimacy with each other and with God (together), a wife wants emotional intimacy (in order to feel ready for physical intimacy), and a husband wants physical intimacy (in order to feel open to emotional vulnerability). What enhances one enhances all. That's why we want to break down the barriers to intimacy and make the art of devotions a win-win-win on all fronts.

There's a great love song right smack-dab in the middle of your Bible. It's a pretty racy love song, and the lyrics are both poetic and potent. It's the beautiful love song of King Solomon. (It's not called the Song of Songs for nothing, you know! The best—and sexiest—song ever!) It's a breathtaking reminder of the joys of intimacy.

It's a beautiful thing, this married love. That's why we've written the following devotions in the spirit of the Song of Solomon, with an eye toward creating legendary, spiritual love.

We can pretty much guarantee that you've never done a couple's devotion like this before, and *you're gonna like it*. Remember, you don't have to do these devotionals in any particular order. If you want to jump around and be random, go ahead. The only rules are that you do the devos as often as you can and that you keep an open heart with the love of your life.

It's fitting that these are the last words of the song "How Do You Keep the Music Playing?":

If we can be the best of lovers, yet be the best of friends

If we can try with every day to make it better as it grows

With any luck then I suppose, the music never ends.

one

Naked and Unashamed

rhythm

Wash some plump, juicy grapes in a colander and bring them bathtub-side. Run a nice bubble bath, light some candles, and set them around the edge of the tub. After you've climbed in together, read on.

listen to the music

The man said,

"This is now bone of my bones
and flesh of my flesh;

she shall be called 'woman,'
for she was taken out of man."

For this reason a man will leave his father and mother and be united to his wife, and they will become one flesh.

The man and his wife were both naked, and they felt no shame. (Gen. 2:23–25 NIV)

what we hear

What would it be like to be the only man and woman alive on the earth? With no one else to compare ourselves to? No rock-hard, airbrushed bodies staring back at us from the magazines. No expectations, no guilt, no shame. What would it feel like to have our lover touch us and not be self-conscious about our pudge or cellulite? What would it be like to be naked and unashamed?

According to a 2006 Body Image Poll conducted by *Fitness* magazine, nearly 20 percent of the women respondents admitted that they have avoided sex at one time or another because they felt uncomfortable with how their bodies looked.[†] (The other 80 percent probably weren't being honest!) The way life is now is most definitely not the way God designed it to be. He was the originator of the First Nudist Colony, and it was a good thing. In Eden we're given a glimpse of a man and woman with not a molecule of shame between them. Unfortunately we humans have a big problem with being attracted to the one thing we're told to avoid, and one bite into forbidden fruit commenced our dance with shame.

But shame is more than skin deep. It can be the result of a lifetime of encounters that have made us feel "less than," inferior, and dirty. These feelings can have absolutely nothing to do with our mate, but our mate picks up the tab for our shame and lack of freedom. Sometimes our nakedness has nothing to do with our state of undress; it may be purely emotional. But often it's when we're most vulnerable that shame can melt away in the embrace of the one whom we feel is most trustworthy. Older couples tell us that failing eyesight and falling body parts coincide, so that should make us all a little more comfortable in our own skin.

what do you hear?

What do the words "one flesh" mean to you?

In the three areas of intimacy (physical, emotional, spiritual), which has you wearing the bigger fig leaf (what you're trying to cover up)? Why?

Fill in the blank: "This year I want to become more free about _____."

extended play

While you're on the journey to becoming naked and unashamed, it might help to consider candles. (Everybody looks better in candlelight, right?) Face your lover with a confident smile (preferably wearing only a smile) and offer lots of reassuring words. (That goes for both of you!) Vow to do everything you can to make your relationship your own personal Eden—a No Shame Zone.

---

† http://www.fitnessmagazine.com/fitness/story.jhtml?storyid=/templatedata/fitness/story/data/1146252364875.xml. (Accessed May 4, 2007.)

two

Sniff This

rhythm

Share a cup of a hot, steamy beverage. (That's one cup, for two.)

listen to the music

While the king was at his table,
  my perfume spread its fragrance.

My lover is to me a sachet of myrrh
  resting between my breasts.

My lover is to me a cluster of henna blossoms
  from the vineyards of En Gedi. (Song 1:12–14 NIV)

what we hear

They say that olfactory memory is the most sensate—meaning a smell can immediately put you back in a certain place or time. If you smell newly sharpened pencils and Elmer's glue, you will be instantly transported to the first day of first grade. The smell of roast and potatoes in the oven can take you back to Sunday dinner at your grandma's house. The smell of cotton candy can put you right back at the 1976 state fair. Bottom line: The nose knows. In the time of Solomon, perfumes and oils were personal signature scents. But you've probably noticed that a perfume or cologne can mix with a person's chemistry so that it smells completely different from one person to another. We all have our own essence, and even newborns can distinguish between their own mother's smell (eau de Mama) and that of a stranger. Widows and widowers will almost universally refer to missing their mate's smell—and they will sleep with articles of clothing that retain that special aroma or will be overcome with grief when they catch a whiff of someone wearing their spouse's brand of cologne or perfume. We have today to breathe each other in, literally. It's a privilege of intimacy to nuzzle up and appreciate the unique aroma of each other.

what do you hear?

If both of you were blindfolded, and neither of you was allowed to wear a fragrance, do you think you could identify each other by scent alone?

What scent makes you think only of your lover?

To what scent would you compare your spouse?

extended play

Do you have a special scent for your bedroom (e.g., candle, incense, cinnamon potpourri)? Maybe now is the time to choose a singular scent that becomes your signature bedroom aroma.

three

Can't Buy Me Love

rhythm

Plunk yourselves down in front of a page of the classified ads. See who can find the most bizarre item for sale.

listen to the music

Hang my locket around your neck,
wear my ring on your finger.

Love is invincible facing danger and death.
Passion laughs at the terrors of hell.

The fire of love stops at nothing—
it sweeps everything before it.

Flood waters can't drown love,
torrents of rain can't put it out.

Love can't be bought, love can't be sold—
it's not to be found in the marketplace. (Song 8:6–7)

what we hear

Russell Conwell's speech "Acres of Diamonds" tells of a young man who went in search of his fortune only to die in the pursuit and have someone else discover that the diamonds were in his backyard all along. The story strikes us as doubly tragic because he had wasted all that energy and time and traded his life trying to find something that was, literally, in his possession to begin with.

We live in a time when some couples casually marry and then just as readily abandon commitments and vows as they strike out to find their "true soul mate," only to discover that the relationship they're looking for is the one they just threw away. The Scripture from Song of Solomon invokes the power and passion of a single-minded, single-hearted love that's determined to survive the inevitable storms of life. This kind of love can't be bought or sold because it's priceless. This passion can't be found elsewhere in the marketplace of life—not in the classified ads, not on QVC ("only six easy installments!"). If you find yourself wondering whether another person could fulfill your needs more completely than your spouse, it's likely you're inaccurately appraising the unique and priceless relationship you already have. Anyone can find a handy slicer-dicer on an infomercial, but a committed, passionate love can't be bought or sold. It's something all the world longs for yet can't seem to find. But it's something we can possess with our spouses if we truly seek it and nurture it.

what do you hear?

What symbols of love do you wear on a regular basis (such as a wedding band, a locket, or a tattoo)?

If money were no object, what would you give your spouse as a symbol of your never-ending love?

If your house were on fire, your loved ones were safe from harm, and you only had time to grab one memento of your love, what would it be? Why?

extended play

Your love is one of a kind, so express it by giving each other specific personal items that are unique to your love story. That way you can keep a symbol of your priceless love within your view daily.

four

Christmas Every Day

rhythm

Find two self-adhesive gift-wrap bows and attach one to each other. (You decide where to affix them.) Wear them for at least the next ten minutes.

listen to the music

But each one is tempted when, by his own evil desire, he is dragged away and enticed. Then, after desire has conceived, it gives birth to sin; then sin, when it is full-grown, gives birth to death.

Don't be deceived, my dear brothers. Every good and perfect gift is from above, coming down from the Father of the heavenly lights, who does not change like shifting shadows. (James 1:14–17 NIV)

what we hear

Bill Murray starred in a movie called *Groundhog Day,* which is about a guy who gets stuck in the same day over and over again. He figures out after awhile that he'll never escape the cycle until he loses his narcissistic ways and learns to recognize the little things that make life worth living.

Let's face it: There are certain elements of existence that can make our day-to-day lives together less than stimulating. Without ever intending to, we can get caught up in our own personal "groundhog days," where it feels like we're just living the same day over and over—no surprises—and it all seems a little too familiar. In our mates we've certainly been given a good gift, but like any gift, when the newness wears off, we can take our relationship for granted. We would readily admit that neither of us is a "perfect" gift, but we can be good and perfect for each other. We've all seen those couples who still live together but barely acknowledge one another, much less appreciate each other. There's a lot to be said about the comfort and familiarity of marriage as long as it doesn't turn into laziness and apathy.

Remember the Journey song "Faithfully" where Steve Perry sings "I get the joy of rediscovering you"? It's easy to think that you have nothing new to discover about your love, but we all change from week to week and year to year. If we let the *Groundhog Day* syndrome bury us in the more tedious, repetitive tasks of life, we can lose our appreciation for each other. Unwrap and enjoy your gift every day.

what do you hear?

Imagine you're opening each other like a present. Describe what attributes of the gift you're most excited about.

When you were younger and dreaming of the gift God would bring you in a mate, what did you dream about?

In what way(s) does your spouse surpass your dreams and expectations?

extended play
Give God thanks for the "good and perfect gift" of your spouse—then open your present!

five

Tied Up in Knots

rhythm

Get knotted up—seriously intertwined. Arms and fingers and legs and ankles. Then read on.

listen to the music

Two are better than one because they have a good return for their labor. For if either of them falls, the one will lift up his companion. But woe to the one who falls when there is not another to lift him up. Furthermore, if two lie down together they keep warm, but how can one be warm alone? And if one can overpower him who is alone, two can resist him. A cord of three strands is not quickly torn apart. (Eccl. 4:9–12 NASB)

what we hear

If you ask most singles what they long for when they think of being in a relationship, they'll most likely respond, "Someone to share life with." An old adage says, "With two, joys are doubled, and sorrows are halved." Yes, it's sappy, but it's also true. Most everything is better when you have someone to share it with. When we're apart, we'll even call each other to discuss what we're looking at, just because we wish the other person was there to share it ("The wind is blowing the snow around, and it looks like a snow globe" or "I wish you could see this sunset"). We love that we have different strengths and weaknesses and that, between us, there's a pretty good balance all around. This isn't to say that our differences don't become annoying (do not stop at this point and discuss your list of grievances with your spouse!), it's just that over the course of time, we keep each other somewhat on track. This would be a great dynamic alone, but the wisdom from Ecclesiastes tells us that people who are married and have a personal faith have a stronger strand in their relationship—a third strand that has no weaknesses and makes the couple exponentially stronger than it would be separately or together: God. His strength is our strength, our joys are greater because of his blessing, and our sorrows are diminished because we can place our cares on his strong shoulders. His love makes our love invincible.

what do you hear?

What strengths do you think your spouse brings to the marriage?

Has there been a time in your marriage when, except for the strength of the third strand, you wouldn't have hung in there?

Describe a specific time in the last month when your mate was there for you and made you feel stronger.

extended play

Pray with each other and thank God for some specific strengths you're grateful for in your mate. Also, thank God for the times he's kept you together.

With Ownership Comes Privilege

rhythm

Come together anywhere there is running water—near a garden hose, near a waterfall, or in the shower …

listen to the music

Do you know the saying, "Drink from your own rain barrel,
 draw water from your own spring-fed well"?

It's true. Otherwise, you may one day come home
 and find your barrel empty and your well polluted.

Your spring water is for you and you only,
 not to be passed around among strangers.

Bless your fresh-flowing fountain!
 Enjoy the wife you married as a young man!

Lovely as an angel, beautiful as a rose—
 don't ever quit taking delight in her body.

Never take her love for granted!

Why would you trade enduring intimacies for cheap thrills
*   with a whore?*
*   for dalliance with a promiscuous stranger?*

Mark well that God doesn't miss a move you make;
*   he's aware of every step you take. (Prov. 5:15–21)*

I have come into my garden, my sister, my bride;
*   I have gathered my myrrh with my spice.*

I have eaten my honeycomb and my honey;
*   I have drunk my wine and my milk. (Song 5:1a NIV)*

what we hear

Solomon certainly seemed to enjoy that word *my*. It was all his, and he was happy to say so.

We were privileged to take a trip of a lifetime last year. We went to Italy for a couple of weeks to celebrate our twenty-fifth wedding anniversary. It was a beautiful time spent in a beautiful country. When we were in Rome, we noticed the strangest thing: People didn't throw away their empty water bottles but would carry them around. We thought this was very odd until we figured out what they were doing. They were refilling them from the various free-flowing fountains that were built centuries ago and are still providing pristine water everywhere in Rome. The water supply to these fountains is clean and pure and in constant supply. That was a revelation to us, since in the United States we can't get clean-tasting water out of pipes that are only ten years old.

Our twenty-five-year mark isn't that amazing compared to some other couples, but we can't believe it's been this long. Our love is sweeter than ever, and it only continues to get better. With ownership comes privilege—to love one person and to commit your life to creating memories with him or her.

The writer of Proverbs tells us, "Never take her love for granted," because with the passing years may also come the temptation to believe that you'll always have each other. This leads to stagnant water, and you know what that breeds—insect larvae and pond scum! It's the closed nature of married love that makes it so sacred, and the moving, free-flowing nature of this relationship that keeps us refreshed through the years.

what do you hear?

What are some things in your relationship that have only improved with age?

What are a couple of areas where you might take each other for granted?

What are some safeguards you can build into your marriage to protect your "spring-fed well"?

extended play

When referring to each other in public, try attaching the possessive "my" in front of your love's name. Revel in your ownership.

seven

The Eyes Have It

rhythm

Make a date to go out to dinner and take this book with you. If that's not possible, at least sit across the table from each other at home—where you can make eyes at each other.

listen to the music

As an apricot tree stands out in the forest,
my lover stands above the young men in town.

All I want is to sit in his shade,
to taste and savor his delicious love.

He took me home with him for a festive meal but his eyes
feasted on me! (Song 2:3–4)

what we hear

Isn't it interesting to look around a restaurant and try to guess how long a couple has been together? It's pretty obvious who's new and who's not. The newly minted lovers are gazing deeply into each other's eyes and hanging on to every word that drops from their beloved's mouth. Those who have been on the field a little longer are casually glancing around as they converse, bringing their focus back to their partner every now and again. Those who are vets are usually the easiest to spot. They're looking anywhere but at each other and have absolutely nothing to say that isn't related to the condition of their entrée. When it comes to a woman feeling intimacy, guys, the eyes have it. It's one of the primary rules of sports: "Keep your eye on the ball" or "Look where you're throwing." Because where the eyes focus, the hands follow, thus the term *hand-eye coordination*. You probably knew this intuitively as a date-r, but you may have lost touch with this concept as a mate-r. Not that we're giving away a trade secret here, but chicks dig the prolonged gaze into the eyes. So much so that if you haven't done it for a while, your beloved will feel something so intense that she'll probably look away. But you'll be rewarded for what it does for her soul as soon as you can get the waiter to bring the check.

what do you hear?

Estimate the amount of time you spent gazing into each other's eyes daily when you were dating. About how much time do you spend eyeball to eyeball these days? More than ten minutes? Less than one?

What do you think accounts for the change?

Try to lock into a gaze with your mate. How long do you think you could look into each other's eyes before you giggle or break the stare? If the eyes are indeed "the windows to the soul," perhaps you both need a little more time looking "into" each other instead of "at" each other.

extended play

Plan an evening at a quiet restaurant with the intention of making everyone else in the place guesstimate that you're newly dating based on your eye contact alone.

eight

Is the Bar Too High?

rhythm

Spread out a few magazines on the floor and play the "let-the-pages-fall-open" game. See how many ads are designed to fuel your personal discontent.

listen to the music

After looking at the way things are on this earth, here's what I've decided is the best way to live: Take care of yourself, have a good time, and make the most of whatever job you have for as long as God gives you life. And that's about it. That's the human lot. Yes, we should make the most of what God gives, both the bounty and the capacity to enjoy it, accepting what's given and delighting in the work. It's God's gift! God deals out joy in the present, the now. (Eccl. 5:18–20)

what we hear

Raise the bar! Kick it up a notch or two! Do more, be more, have more! Get with the program! The Joneses are winning the rat race!

We live in a society with an entire advertising industry

devoted to making us feel an intense underlying discontentment with our lives. It's insidious, ubiquitous (look it up). We get caught up in the comparison trap and wonder why the little things just don't give us the same level of "juice" we used to feel.

In Ecclesiastes we're brought back to the most basic elements of life: You have a family, you have food, you have meaningful work. If we're waiting for something to happen tomorrow that will bring us more joy, or if we're thinking that things were so much better in the past, we're caught in a place where joy can't live. This passage of Scripture says that real joy is "in the present, the now." So what's up with your kvetching? This life *and the capacity to enjoy it* are both gifts from God. When it comes to the expectations department, instead of constantly raising the bar, we may need to lower it. It's not an issue of settling for less but of savoring God's gifts more.

what do you hear?

Are you more prone to dwell on the past or to worry about the future? What letter grade would you give yourselves (and each other) for your skill at living fully in the present?

Relate areas of your life where you've succumbed to comparison and ingratitude.

In what specific ways can you help each other tune into simple everyday pleasures and joys?

extended play

Make a pact to catch each other when one or the other is losing touch with the Enjoyment Element. Keep a running list of "Simple Things That Bring Him or Her Joy," and try to do a couple each week. In the South we call these small pleasures *Happies*.

nine

Sweet Nothings

rhythm

Pull out your cell phones and dial each other up, even if you're only sitting twelve inches apart. Listen to the delay as your voice pings off a satellite somewhere and then bounces back to earth. Try to imagine the points of potential disconnect that could occur on that path from your mouth to your mate's ear and back again.

listen to the music

> You've captured my heart, dear friend.
>> You looked at me, and I fell in love.
>> One look my way and I was hopelessly in love!
>
> How beautiful your love, dear, dear friend—
>> far more pleasing than a fine, rare wine …
>> every syllable you speak a delicacy to savor. (Song 4:9–11)

what we hear

Do you remember when you were first in love, and you just couldn't wait to hear what your beloved was about to say? You didn't want to miss a word. Every syllable was brilliant! Enchanting! Full of meaning! You would talk for hours about everything and nothing at all.

Then somewhere between "I do" and "Did you remember to pick up the dry cleaning?" you entered something known as the Marriage Communication Drop-Out Zone, where the most common message is "Can you hear me now?"

We find ourselves asking each other to repeat things not so much because we're going deaf, but because we aren't really listening. Part of the problem may be that the words we're saying to each other are only designed to impart information, not to connect us on a heart level or to communicate love to each other. Finding the path back to the idea that the words your lover speaks are sweet—regardless of the content—requires a commodity you had in spades when you were dating but is hard to come by in the workaday, work-it-out world: your undivided attention.

what do you hear?

What do you love to hear your lover say to you?

Imagine that one of you is called away on a long-term job assignment or into military service, and a voice on the phone might be all you had to connect you. What would you say to each other?

When was the last time you whispered something intimate to your lover?

extended play

Make a point to call your mate at least once a day just for "sweet nothings"—a little audible flirting. Make sure you close your office door or turn off the speaker on your phone. (And make sure you dial the right number!)

ten

Don't Miss the Moment

rhythm

Look at your watches. Do they read the same time—to the minute? If not, synchronize them.

listen to the music

I was sound asleep, but in my dreams I was wide awake.
  Oh, listen! It's the sound of my lover knocking, calling!

[The Man] "Let me in, dear companion, dearest friend,
  my dove, consummate lover!

I am soaked with the dampness of the night,
  drenched with dew, shivering and cold."

[The Woman] "But I'm in my nightgown—do you expect me
  to get dressed?
  I'm bathed and in bed—do you want me to get dirty?"

But my lover wouldn't take no for an answer,
  and the longer he knocked, the more excited I became.

I got up to open the door to my lover,
  sweetly ready to receive him,

Desiring and expectant
* as I turned the door handle.*

But when I opened the door he was gone.
* My loved one had tired of waiting and left.*

And I died inside—oh, I felt so bad! (Song 5:2–6)

what we hear

Do we really need to comment on one person being *out* of the mood when the other person is *in* the mood? We see from the Scripture passage that the list of excuses began several hundred centuries ago. "I'm already in bed." "My feet will get dirty." "I have a headache." And as much as this seems like a male-knocking, female-rebuffing scenario, timing is everything, and it can definitely work both ways (or not work, as the case may be). When you get down to it, almost any time is the right time; it just depends on whether we perceive it to be *convenient* or *ideal*. But so what if it's inconvenient? And since when is it such a bad thing to be desired? What *is* bad is forgetting that you are lovers, first and foremost. It would be a shame if tomorrow was the last day of your life, and you missed your last chance to make passionate love to your spouse. So ditch the potential regret and open the door already.

what do you hear?

What do you think your mate hears when you say, "I'm just not in the mood"?

What would help you get in the mood—or stay there?

Has there ever been a time (maybe many!) when you *thought* you weren't in the mood, but once you got into it, you really were? Discuss the occurrence.

extended play

Planned spontaneity: seems like an oxymoron, but it's not. Agree on a night or two of the week designated as the No Rejection Zone, when lovemaking is on the calendar—anticipated, planned for. This doesn't preclude making love more often; it just makes it an event to look forward to with regularity.

eleven

A Little Flirting Goes a Long Way

rhythm

Find your first photo album. (You do have all your pictures neatly arranged in albums, right?) Turn to (or dig out of the shoebox) a picture of you two when you were dating. Can you recall when every encounter was a flirtfest?

listen to the music

> *[The Man] Oh, my dear friend! You're so beautiful!*
> *And your eyes so beautiful—like doves!*

> *[The Woman] And you, my dear lover—you're so handsome!*
> *And the bed we share is like a forest glen.*

> *We enjoy a canopy of cedars*
> *enclosed by cypresses, fragrant and green.*

> *I'm just a wildflower picked from the plains of Sharon,*
> *a lotus blossom from the valley pools.*

> *[The Man] A lotus blossoming in a swamp of weeds—*

that's my dear friend among the girls of the village.
(Song 1:15—2:2)

what we hear

We'd like to take flirting back! It has been confiscated by teenagers
and dating singles and almost abandoned by the people who could
elevate it to an art form: married lovers. Compliments with a flirty
edge keep the heart young and the love fresh. And who doesn't long
to hear that their beloved still finds them attractive?

It may be a little difficult to remember, but there was definitely a time in your courtship history when you would rehearse a
flirty exchange to yourself for hours before delivering your line.
You would imagine yourself saying it and then imagine what the
response would be. Flirting had forethought and was a strong
warm-up that led to the serious potential for kissing and hugging.

Here in Solomon's exchange with his beloved, the girl
exclaims, "I'm just plain!" (Guys, can you hear the Zebco line
zinging out there, just waiting for you to take the bait?) He
responds, "No way! You are so much better looking than the other
girls." To which, we can only imagine, she bats her eyes and melts
a little and then invites him back under the canopy of cedars and
cypresses for some R & R.

what do you hear?

Which type of flirting do you most enjoy? Flirting with your eyes?
Your hands? Your words?

When did you last flirt with your mate when you were in a crowded place?

Do you two have a secret signal that lets the other know, "Let's get out of here"? If not, come up with one now and look forward to using it soon!

extended play

Flirty text messaging isn't just for teenagers. Reclaim it as your own.

twelve

Perpetual Springtime

rhythm

Find some flowers—real ones would be nice, but silk ones will do. Make a couple out of tissue paper if you must. Put them between you.

listen to the music

My lover has arrived
and he's speaking to me!

Get up, my dear friend,
fair and beautiful lover—come to me!

Look around you: Winter is over;
the winter rains are over, gone!

Spring flowers are in blossom all over.
The whole world's a choir—and singing!

Spring warblers are filling the forest
with sweet arpeggios.

Lilacs are exuberantly purple and perfumed
and cherry trees fragrant with blossoms.

Oh, get up, dear friend,
    my fair and beautiful lover—come to me!
    (Song 2:10–13)

what we hear

For people who live in Arizona, this line will mean nothing, but for residents of North Dakota, it will mean everything. In the movie *The Lion, the Witch and the Wardrobe,* the half-man, half-faun character named Tumnus tells Lucy that the White Witch has cast a spell on Narnia: "It's she that makes it always winter. Always winter and never Christmas; think of that!"

Can you imagine a more bleak existence? Some marriages can become like that—cold and joyless. But spring—just the name of the season evokes thoughts of newness and life. It's the time, as Alfred, Lord Tennyson wrote, when "a young man's fancy lightly turns to thoughts of love." Perpetual springtime is all in the mind; it's how you view your love. Do you mentally picture your lover as dormant and chilly or vibrant and evergreen, worthy of renewal and celebration? Whatever season your marriage may be in, you can keep the springtime in your heart. Flowers are an any-season gift of love for a reason: They're beautiful, bright, and reminders of spring. If you're in love with your spouse, every day can be springtime, and it can always be Easter.

what do you hear?

What kinds of flowers speak to you? Do you have a favorite?

To what flower would you compare your love?

Springtime is also a time for cleaning. What kinds of behaviors could you afford to "clean out" of your relationship?

extended play

Rose petals strewn in a bath or on a bed are beautiful in *any* season.

thirteen

The Spice of a Spontaneous Getaway

rhythm

Your choice—just so you can show off your spontaneity.

listen to the music

I belong to my lover,
  and his desire is for me.

Come, my lover, let us go to the countryside,
  let us spend the night in the villages.

Let us go early to the vineyards
  to see if the vines have budded,
  if their blossoms have opened,
  and if the pomegranates are in bloom—
  there I will give you my love.

The mandrakes send out their fragrance,
  and at our door is every delicacy,
  both new and old,
  that I have stored up for you, my lover. (Song 7:10–13 NIV)

what we hear

Do you hear what the woman is saying? "Hey, babe. Grab your toothbrush and pretty much nothing else. We're outta here! I've arranged a babysitter, and we're driving out to the country for a quick getaway—just you and me and some room service." A night in the country with delicacies "stored up for you."

A romantic getaway can be initiated by a husband or a wife, but the key is that it transmits *forethought*. This especially speaks to a woman's heart. In fact, we might say it like this: Anytime a husband uses forethought, a woman appreciates it in the same way that he appreciates foreplay. When a guy takes the lead—even if it's just to get a college student to stay overnight with the kids so he and his wife can go up the road to a bed and breakfast with some room service (especially for a woman who is a mother and has to plan the meals and the vacation and the orthodontist appointments, or a career woman who needs to be pampered occasionally)—and he says, "I've already planned it; I want to be alone with you," a woman thinks, *I've won the romance lottery. I'm worth the time it took for him to plan this. I'm treasured. I'm taken care of.* And it's not just a girl thing! When a woman "kidnaps" her man and takes him to a place where the main event is some intentional physical intimacy, he thinks, *Wow! She still desires me and wants to be alone with me.*

Talk about creating some space for romance and intimacy— woo-hoo! These types of encounters keep passion fresh and allow time to recharge emotionally. And know this: Even the shortest adventures beat no adventures at all.

what do you hear?

What was the last completely spontaneous, crazy thing you did together?

Who is the more spontaneous one in your relationship?

Why is this type of quick getaway a necessity? How does it make you feel?

extended play

There are probably thirty places within fifty miles of you—no matter where you live—that are quick getaway options. All it takes is some forethought and a minimum of planning; so don't just think about it, *do it!*

fourteen

It's the Thoughts That Count

rhythm

Meet up in the bathroom—or wherever you keep your perfume and body lotions.

listen to the music

Let him kiss me with the kisses of his mouth—
*   for your love is more delightful than wine.*

Pleasing is the fragrance of your perfumes;
*   your name is like perfume poured out.*
*   No wonder the maidens love you!*

Take me away with you—let us hurry!
*   Let the king bring me into his chambers.*
*   (Song 1:1–4 NIV)*

what we hear

When we were younger, a Heinz Ketchup commercial celebrated the waiting time one had to endure to get the thick, rich ketchup out of the bottle. Heinz's theme song? Carly Simon's

"Anticipation." If you've ever stared at a bottle of ketchup just hoping that something would move toward your fries, you know that song doesn't lie. But the concept of anticipation only works if you're looking forward to something.

When you think of being with your mate—just chillin' or engaged in a project or in some other activity—do you anticipate being together? Does the thought itself bring you joy? This Scripture from Song of Solomon reminds us that anticipation is great fuel when we're apart. And the journey toward being intimate on every level involves nurturing our thoughts about each other when we're apart. When you're away from your lover, do you spend time considering his or her attributes? Are you anticipating a great encounter or just another ho-hum, same old, same old?

In the movie *Don Juan DeMarco,* Marlon Brando's character, a psychiatrist, had settled into a long case of romantic blahs until he treats a delusional patient who thinks he's Don Juan, the greatest lover in the world. After awhile, Brando's character begins to see himself as a great lover to his wife, and doggone it, he becomes one. As a man (or woman) thinks in his (or her) heart, so is he (or she). (See Prov. 23:7 NKJV.) Anticipation can be sweet.

what do you hear?

What thoughts about your mate occupy your mind when you're apart?

Do you sometimes get lost in thoughts about your mate's attributes and/or in the anticipation of your next romantic encounter?

Could you say any of the lines from today's Scripture to your spouse and truly mean it, or would you just crack up because you don't see yourself as the "romantic" type?

extended play

If you're truly interested in making your love last for your lifetime, it will take personal resolve to be the best lover there has ever been. Maybe it's time to step up your game in the romance department. Make a personal vow that no one on earth will outlove you.

fifteen

Home Security Systems

rhythm

Check that all the doors are locked. Check again—I think I heard something. Then enfold your woman safe in your arms.

listen to the music

Then you must protect me from the foxes,
    foxes on the prowl,

Foxes who would like nothing better
    than to get into our flowering garden. (Song 2:15)

Keep vigilant watch over your heart;
    that's where life starts.

Don't talk out of both sides of your mouth;
    avoid careless banter, white lies and gossip.

Keep your eyes straight ahead;
    ignore all sideshow attractions.

Watch your step,
    and the road will stretch out smooth before you.

Look neither right nor left;
    leave evil in the dust. (Prov. 4:23–27)

what we hear

When we were in Venice, Italy, we went to an artisan glassblowing demonstration on the island of Murano. The glassworkers would take some sand and heat it up, then they'd twist and shape the newly formed glass until they had created "leetle horses." After the demo they took us to a showroom to try to sell us some "leetle horses" for a *lotta* money. They were "leetle" *and* expensive.

It's not hard to understand why you would want to guard your garden against gorillas. Anyone could see a gorilla coming and would know that he would get into that garden, jump around, trample the flowers, jerk up the vines, and basically make a mess of the place. But little foxes? Hey, they're cute. And they seem pretty harmless. The most they could do is nip a little with their teeth. Where's the harm in that? Not much, unless you look up one day and find that those "leetle foxes" have cost you more than you were willing to pay.

We're pretty sure that not too many people wake up one day and say to themselves, "Hey, I know what I'm gonna do! I'm gonna start a rip-roaring illicit affair, so I can decimate my family and ruin a lot of people's lives. That sounds like a great idea!" It usually starts out rather harmlessly with those "leetle foxes." So set up your home security system with your lover and make sure that you keep the foxes of "careless banter, white lies and gossip" out of your garden.

what do you hear?

What are the "leetle foxes" in your marriage? What little things erode your time together and attention to each other on a daily basis?

In what ways can you partner together to protect your garden? Might it require more vigilance around your daily schedule?

Are you involved in any commitments or relationships that don't further the cause of your home and family? What could (or should) go?

extended play

Make a pact with your mate to always confess to each other any ongoing attraction you might have for someone else. By doing this, you'll ensure there's no secretive or salacious nature to the attraction. The confession might also open up a chance to discuss the little foxes that could otherwise turn into giant gorillas.

sixteen

The Original Secret Garden

rhythm

If you have a garden, go there. If you have to sneak over to your neighbors' garden, make sure they aren't members of the National Rifle Association. Or if you just have find a nice secluded patch of lawn, that will do.

listen to the music

[The Man] Dear lover and friend, you're a secret garden,
*   a private and pure fountain.*

Body and soul, you are paradise,
*   a whole orchard of succulent fruits—*

Ripe apricots and peaches,
*   oranges and pears;*

Nut trees and cinnamon,
*   and all scented woods;*

Mint and lavender,
*   and all herbs aromatic;*

A garden fountain, sparkling and splashing,
*   fed by spring waters from the Lebanon mountains.*

[The Woman] Wake up, North Wind,
  get moving, South Wind!

Breathe on my garden,
  fill the air with spice fragrance.

Oh, let my lover enter his garden!
  Yes, let him eat the fine, ripe fruits. (Song 4:12–16)

what we hear

Isn't it great to know a secret nobody else knows? It makes you feel a little smug (in a good way). That's one of the beauties of monogamy—your marriage, your intimacy, is your garden. Yours alone. No one else knows the layout or the wonders of your garden. Singer and songwriter John Mayer performs a song titled "Your Body is a Wonderland," and you have to wonder if Solomon was humming the tune as he described his lover. It was as if Solomon was dictating the layout of his secret garden to let his woman know that he was aware of each enjoyable section. She was a refreshing fountain, his alone—body and soul. This is instructive to us as lovers, since sometimes it's easy to give the body but a little more difficult to reveal the soul. But true intimacy requires that we allow each other full access to both.

Solomon's lover was every tree in the orchard, and every sweet-smelling herb. She was all that and a bag of chips. And notice her response: willingness in spades! "Come on in, this garden is for you." Original love began with a man and a woman in a secret garden. We've been trying to get back there ever since.

what do you hear?

Are you tending your "garden," or has it been largely ignored and become overgrown with weeds? (Familiarity can breed personal-hygiene laziness.)

Ask your love what one thing you could do that would make your "garden" a more succulent place for him or her.

What is your favorite place in your secret garden?

extended play

Tend to your garden! Physical activity of almost any kind enhances our stamina, so this might be a good time to commit to some sort of regular exercise together. (It could be as simple as taking a stroll after dinner or hitting the YMCA together twice a week.)

seventeen

On the Same Page

rhythm

Bring the coffee or orange juice back to bed this morning and read on.

listen to the music

So, my dear friends, listen carefully;
    those who embrace these my ways are most blessed.

Mark a life of discipline and live wisely;
    don't squander your precious life.

Blessed the man, blessed the woman, who listens to me,
    awake and ready for me each morning,
    alert and responsive as I start my day's work.

When you find me, you find life, real life,
    to say nothing of God's good pleasure. (Prov. 8:32–35)

what we hear

One of us isn't a morning person. The other one has learned to accommodate that. Probably one of you isn't a morning person either, but there's something to the idea of getting up on the right side of the bed, somehow getting in sync before the day is too far gone (although our definitions of what time that actually is might differ). We spend a lot of our married lives wishing the other person would somehow hop off his or her agenda and get on *our* agenda. But that's not really what God is calling us to. He's asking that both of us align ourselves with *his* agenda, that we be connected to each other and to him and thereby pull together to help each other fulfill our destiny in this time we're living together in. God is asking us to "find where [he] is at work and join him there," as Henry Blackaby so eloquently put it in *Experiencing God*. His desire is for us to live *real* life (sometimes *real*-ly exciting, sometimes *real*-ly difficult) and, in it all, to find God's pleasure. It's not about getting your spouse on *your* page; it's about making sure you're both on God's page.

what do you hear?

How does it feel when you wake up and just know that your partner will be there?

How can you help your spouse prepare for the day and hear God's voice first?

How can we tell that we're on God's page for our lives? What do you engage in each day that makes you feel "God's good pleasure" most? Your work? Your parenthood? Your hobby? Your relationships? Your service?

extended play

Go against typecasting! Make Monday morning your new favorite morning of the week together—get up a little earlier, look over your schedules for the week and pray about them, help each other plan your priorities, (and adjust your schedules accordingly), and maybe take a little time for some Monday-morning loving ...

eighteen

Some Cheese with Your Whine?

rhythm

Go to the kitchen, turn on the faucet to a *drip, drip, drip,* and leave it that way until you've finished this devo.

listen to the music

Better a dry crust with peace and quiet
than a house full of feasting, with strife. (Prov. 17:1 NIV)

Better to live alone in a tumbledown shack
than share a mansion with a nagging spouse.
(Prov. 21:9)

Better to live in a tent in the wild
than with a cross and petulant spouse. (Prov. 21:19)

A nagging spouse is like
the drip, drip, drip of a leaky faucet;

You can't turn it off,
and you can't get away from it.
(Prov. 27:15–16)

what we hear

Peace is hard to come by in our world. It's hard to find globally, it's hard to find at work, and sometimes it's impossible to find in our own homes. If we feel we aren't being heard or understood, we'll often ratchet up the noise and the frequency until we get the level of acknowledgment we're looking for. At least that's one explanation. Another is that nagging is just a very bad out-of-control habit. Regardless of the reason for the noise, the effect is still the same: *drip, drip, drip, drip, drip, drip, drip.* It's annoying just to read it, much less listen to it.

Women have an intense desire for connection, and if they aren't getting it in a peaceful way, they'll try another way. Men have a deep desire to fix things and solve problems, so they'll harp on a logical solution in their effort to communicate their concerns. The proverbs in the previous section are trying to communicate something in four different ways, and the message is this: Nagging doesn't work! Quite the opposite. It causes your spouse to tune you out entirely in his or her quest for peace.

You're an ambassador for peace in your own universe: your home. No drips allowed.

what do you hear?

Confess one of your "drip" issues—the thing you bring up on a daily basis, sometimes multiple times a day. Not that it's news to your spouse, but recognition on your part is the first step toward change.

What method do you use for emphasis when you feel you aren't being heard? Repetition? Volume? The silent treatment?

What sort of signal can you give to each other when the *drip, drip, drip* is just about to get on your very last nerve?

extended play

Take several index cards and write your "drip" issues on them, maybe using only one or two words for each. When you feel the need to bring these issues up, make a pact that you won't say them aloud, but you'll go get the card and just hold it up. The point will be made, but you'll have to go to a lot more effort to make it. You'll also make it more pointedly and quietly. Best of all, you might laugh about it instead of feeling your blood pressure going though the roof.

nineteen

"Have Mercy!"

rhythm

Freestyle—you get to pick.

listen to the music

> *Make a clean break with all cutting, backbiting, profane talk. Be gentle with one another, sensitive. Forgive one another as quickly and thoroughly as God in Christ forgave you. (Eph. 4:31–32)*

> *Blessed are the merciful,*
>   *for they will be shown mercy. (Matt. 5:7 NIV)*

what we hear

> *Mercy—n, pl* 1: compassionate or kindly forbearance shown toward an offender, an enemy, or other person in one's power; compassion, pity, or benevolence.

Back a few millennia ago, one of the characters on the sitcom *Full House* would often say, "Have mercy!" when he was referring to a beautiful woman. It got a laugh from the studio audience every time, but in a marriage the ability to muster up feelings of compassion and to show true mercy toward one's mate is nothing to laugh about. Even people with hearts as small as the Grinch's don't find it difficult to feel compassion when they see images of children in other countries who are malnourished and need financial support to survive another day. Yet it's quite another thing to look at our mate, who has done something über-annoying for the 4,447th time this week, and be "moved with compassion." But the truth is this: We all need mercy, and not because we've earned it. It wouldn't be a stretch to say that some of us treat complete strangers with more mercy and compassion than we do our life partners. The Bible refers to maturing believers with terms like "a forbearing spirit" and "longsuffering." Could your tendencies to give mercy to your husband or wife be characterized this way? Be quick to show mercy, as you will surely need it yourself.

what do you hear?

Relate a time recently when you felt particularly compassionate toward your mate (for example, when he or she was having a rough time at work or was sick). Were you moved to show mercy, to do unusually kind things for your spouse because he or she was emotionally or physically weaker than usual?

The concept of *mercy* is "not getting what you deserve." How has experiencing God's mercy in your life made you a more merciful mate? Or has it? (By the way, no piling on the guilt here; that would be very unmerciful!)

Tell each other about a time when a simple act of mercy moved you (not necessarily from your spouse, but just in general).

extended play

As you reflect on the mercies of God, which are "new every morning," according to Lamentations 3, pray together that the God of mercy will renew your mercy for each other every day. Not only that, but that he'll make them "tender mercies." Feel free to lavish them on each other because the divine supply is never ending.

twenty

Banker's Hours

rhythm
Hang out together in your home office or library.

listen to the music
Go ahead and be angry. You do well to be angry—but don't use your anger as fuel for revenge. And don't stay angry. Don't go to bed angry. Don't give the Devil that kind of foothold in your life. (Eph. 4:26–27)

what we hear
On the face of it, this seems pretty un-Christian—this being told to "go ahead and be angry." Doesn't that just contradict all that temperance, forbearance, and self-control stuff? But there it is, bigger than Dallas: "You do well to be angry …" Can that really be biblical?

In reality, couples don't actually "lose" their tempers, they "loose" them. Anger is let out of the cage to wreak havoc for a while, but resentments grow under cover of darkness. A minor scratch becomes a festering wound. Often, the problem is with a woman's imagination. It really isn't that big of a deal to the guy, but the woman can't lay it down. She lies there at night imagining things that may have no grounding in reality, but because they haven't been dealt with, she feels unloved, uncared for—in a word, alone. For the husband, resentment gets driven underground in the "I'm tired, and I'm not going to think about it right now" syndrome. You know, the syndrome that grows ulcers and causes strokes. That's the real issue with the "Don't go to bed angry" admonition, because the "foothold" the Devil gets is in *her mind* and in *his gut*. Better to stay awake another hour and find a place of resolution—or at least a place of respectful disagreement, where love is affirmed regardless of the inability to reach a conclusion that is mutual—than to go to bed with anger and division running loose in the bedroom. You can't afford the repair bill from the damage done overnight, so get anger back in its cage as soon as possible.

what do you hear?

How much time does it take for each of you to get to sleep when there's an unresolved issue between you?

When was the last time you went to bed angry? Has what you were mad about been resolved yet?

We advocate the practice of holding hands while you're arguing, just to reaffirm the fact that a disagreement doesn't mean you're not on the same team. Talk about how this could happen the next time anger is "loosed." Who will be the one to reach out?

extended play

Consider purchasing a book you would love to hear your partner read aloud to you. Soothing words are better than angry ones, right?

interlude one

Let's Stay Together

in•ti•mate in-t*uh*-mit —adj./n.

1. innermost; inward; internal; deep-seated; hearty

2. near; close; direct; thorough; complete

3. close in friendship or acquaintance; familiar; confidential; as, an intimate friend

4. an intimate friend or associate; a confidant

We know that people get married for a variety of reasons: love, lust, companionship, fear of being alone, boredom, financial partnership, neediness, pregnancy. There are as many reasons as there are couples. As your relationship with your spouse has grown, maybe your reasons for staying married aren't the same as the reasons you had for getting married, but you're still together. You are a couple. You are an entity. Now it's a responsibility and a pleasure to get connected and stay connected at the deepest levels.

One of the great attractions of getting married is having someone to share our lives with. Someone we know and who knows us. That means the good, the bad, and the ugly. We all want "connection," but sometimes we're afraid to go all the way there. It's like the intense conflicted feelings in the Dan Hill song: "Sometimes when we touch, the honesty's too much, and I have to close my eyes and hide." We know that intimacy requires us to go to a place where we may be tempted to retreat to a safe place where we're less "exposed." It's easier to stay on the alpha level and reduce our potential risks.

And because of the way God made us as men and women, our definition of *intimacy* will vary wildly. If you poll a group of men, they'll almost always equate the term with the physical. For women, the definition will almost always be verbal and emotional.

That leads to some relationship confusion when we say that we desire more "intimacy." Women don't want any physical connection unless they feel heard. Men don't want to talk unless their sexual needs are met. When a man doesn't feel connected physically to his wife, he'll stop talking. When a woman doesn't feel connected to her husband verbally, she won't respond to him physically. It devolves into something like this:

Woman: "Why won't he talk to me?"

Man: "Why won't she stop talking?"

After awhile the disconnect becomes well established, and the beautiful, God-inspired idea of husband and wife becoming "one flesh" is reduced to just "having sex."

Studies show that a man's best possible outcome after a stressful day is to come home and be quiet for a while. This sounds great until you factor in that a woman's best possible outcome after a stressful day is to come home and talk about it. It seems that our "best possible outcomes" are at odds with each other. So someone is going to be frustrated. But the more we recognize this cavernous difference in the way we define intimacy, the better able we'll be to accommodate and bless each other.

We believe that neither gender sees the whole picture. It's not "either-or;" it's "both-and." If a husband wants a willing lover, he'll *use more words,* and if a wife desires more communication, she'll *use more touch.* This is one of the great messages of the Song of Solomon: The man is a giver of beautiful words; the woman is a giver of her loving touch. *By giving what we'd naturally be tempted to withhold, we receive what we need most.* This requires us to think empathetically, like when we're shopping for a gift. We don't necessarily get what *we* would like; we get what we know would delight the receiver. And the level of effort we put into choosing that gift demonstrates that person's importance to us. If the person is just a passing acquaintance, any old generic gift would do. But the more dear the recipient, the more thought and effort we put into getting just the right thing. Gary Chapman's book *The Five Love Languages* goes into great detail about the different ways our mates receive love. The best gifts are the ones they want, not the ones we want.

Another beautiful aspect of intimacy is that we get to share our life in minute detail with the person we've vowed to love and cherish. We're intimate based on the level of access we are granted to each other. We're living life together and are witnessing it up close and personal. How sad would it be to have had the opportunity to journey through this life together and yet have *never really come to know each other?* The fact that we're committing to having a loving friendship is a gift we give each other every day.

In the movie *Shall We Dance?* Susan Sarandon's character explains why she has chosen to stay married at this point in her life:

> We need a witness to our lives. There's a billion people on the planet… I mean, what does any one life really mean? But in a marriage, you're promising to care about everything. The good things, the bad things, the terrible things, the mundane things … all of it, all of the time, every day. You're saying "Your life will not go unnoticed because I will notice it. Your life will not go un-witnessed because I will be your witness."

True intimacy is the desire to know your mate and to reveal yourself in the process. It requires courage, honesty, and personal investment. It's the difference between marriages that sizzle and marriages that fizzle. It's the difference between your marriage being an original classic or elevator Muzak.

twenty one

Love a Good Mystery?

rhythm

Build a tent with some chairs and blankets like you used to do when you were kids. Get underneath, in the dark, with a flashlight.

listen to the music

Out of respect for Christ, be courteously reverent to one another.

Wives, understand and support your husbands in ways that show your support for Christ. The husband provides leadership to his wife the way Christ does to his church, not by domineering but by cherishing. So just as the church submits to Christ as he exercises such leadership, wives should likewise submit to their husbands.

Husbands, go all out in your love for your wives, exactly as Christ did for the church—a love marked by giving, not getting. Christ's love makes the church whole. His words evoke her beauty. Everything he does and says is designed to bring the best out of her, dressing her in dazzling white silk, radiant with holiness. And that is how husbands ought to love their wives. They're really doing themselves a favor—since they're already "one" in marriage.

No one abuses his own body, does he? No, he feeds and pampers it. That's how Christ treats us, the church, since we are part of his body. And this is why a man leaves father and mother and cherishes his wife. No longer two, they become "one flesh." This is a huge mystery, and I don't pretend to understand it all. What is clearest to me is the way Christ treats the church. And this provides a good picture of how each husband is to treat his wife, loving himself in loving her, and how each wife is to honor her husband. (Eph. 5:21–33)

what we hear

It's a mystery to us, too. As Mark Twain so aptly put it, "It ain't those parts of the Bible that I can't understand that bother me, it is the parts that I do understand." There are parts of this passage that are stunningly clear. How about we just work on those?

what do you hear?

If you were to diagram your marriage, in what ways would it line up with the picture the apostle Paul painted of unity, love, respect, and honor?

What if Christ were to base his church on the way you love each other? Would it be a church you'd want to be a part of? Why or why not?

Of the three concepts discussed in this passage (honor, sacrifice, cherishing), which is the easiest and the hardest for you to express? Why?

extended play

In *The Message* the word *pamper* is used to describe how we treat our bodies (Eph. 5:29). What do you do for each other that could be categorized as pampering? Get out your calendars and write in a *"Pamper Day."* (For those of you with babies still in diapers, that may not have a positive connotation, but try it anyway.) On this day you're responsible for planning one thing that is *your mate's idea of luxury*. You may have to divide the day in half to accomplish sufficient pampering for both of you, but it'll be worth it.

twenty two

I'd Like to Teach *Myself* to Sing

rhythm

Put on a little background music and curl up together on the couch.

listen to the music

Don't fret or worry. Instead of worrying, pray. Let petitions and praises shape your worries into prayers, letting God know your concerns. Before you know it, a sense of God's wholeness, every-thing coming together for good, will come and settle you down. It's wonderful what happens when Christ displaces worry at the center of your life.

Summing it all up, friends, I'd say you'll do best by filling your minds and meditating on things true, noble, reputable, authentic, compelling, gracious—the best, not the worst; the beautiful, not the ugly; things to praise, not things to curse. Put into practice what you learned from me, what you heard and saw and realized. Do that, and God, who makes everything work together, will work you into his most excellent harmonies. (Phil. 4:6–9)

what we hear

We are Marvin Gaye and Tammi Terrell, Roy Rogers and Dale Evans, Peaches and Herb. We're lovers making beautiful music together. But worry stops beautiful music dead in its tracks. To put it plainly, worry is a thief. It robs us of focus and faith—and parks itself square between us and our view of The Great Conductor. We might be reading the same score, but we'll be continuously offbeat if we can't see his leading. Experts tell us that the best dancers never worry about their feet, and the best singers never think about hitting the notes. They just do what they've trained to do.

During the winter Olympics, we love to watch the ice-dancing competitions. The skaters take turns skating forward and backward, yet they're always together, always in step. If they take a tumble, they tumble together—and it's usually painful to watch. The duet is continuous, and when it's working, it's a beautiful thing.

When our minds are filled with higher thoughts, we leave little emotional energy for worrying, which means we can see our musical scores more clearly and the downbeats God orchestrates for our lives. And when it's working, baby, it's a beautiful thing!

what do you hear?

If you sliced out a random twenty-minute segment of your average day, about how many minutes would be spent in thoughts that could be categorized as "worry" thoughts (anxieties about the past, the future, your kids, your job, your finances)?

What role do you think your gender plays in worrying?

What can you do about replacing your thoughts of worry with the kinds of thoughts Paul listed in Philippians? (Or would that be a new category of worry: worrying about how much you worry?)

extended play

Write the better thoughts Paul listed on a couple of Post-it Notes and put them where you spend time. (Read: "Places where your mind is most likely to wander toward worry," such as on the dashboard of your car or on your bathroom mirror) Practice shaping your "worries into prayers" and letting God's peace rule in your hearts and minds.

twenty three

Dancing Lessons

rhythm

Go to a place with some tunes and some space, and "cut a rug" with your lover. (For all you twentysomethings out there, to "cut a rug" means "dance.")

listen to the music

Let them praise his name in dance;
  strike up the band and make great music!

And why? Because God delights in his people,
  festoons plain folk with salvation garlands!

Let true lovers break out in praise,
  sing out from wherever they're sitting. (Ps. 149:3–5)

what we hear

Because we both grew up Baptist, we have very little dancing history. Maybe it's for the best, as neither of us dances very well. (We believe that over the generations, all the dancing genes may have been bred out of us.) It's just plain funny when we try, but that doesn't mean we don't do it. In fact, the older we get, the less we care what anybody thinks about our dancing skills. Dancing and golf are in the same category: You don't have to be good to enjoy the activity.

In the movie *Footloose,* Kevin Bacon's character uses verses from the Bible to convince a nondancing town that God considers a dance in his honor a high form of praise. Have you ever felt so happy about something that you just spontaneously broke into a "happy dance"? I'm thinking specifically about wide receivers in the end zone, the last out of the final baseball game in the World Series, or any woman finding a cute pair of shoes in her size on the 75 percent off sales rack. God loves it when we're so excited about him that we can't contain it and simply have to dance our praise. It's also wonderful to celebrate our love for our spouse with a dance. In Lee Ann Womack's hit song "I Hope You Dance," she sings about the potential for regret when we sit out the dances life brings our way. Happy dance, boogie, salsa, or swing—there's something enchanting in the moment we decide to take the chance and dance.

what do you hear?

When was the last time you personally did a little "happy dance"?

When, if ever, have you danced in worship to God?

What keeps you from dancing more than you do?

extended play

No matter how spastic you may be on the dance floor, *e-v-e-r-y-b-o-d-y* can slow-dance. It's basically a long rhythmic hug. And if you have two left feet, just keep shuffling both of them along while you engage in some deep eye contact with your partner. Turn down the lights, turn up your special song, and go for it!

twenty four

It's All Your Fault

rhythm

Hide in the closet. (If you both have a closet and one of them is cleaner, go there.)

listen to the music

When they heard the sound of God strolling in the garden in the evening breeze, the Man and his Wife hid in the trees of the garden, hid from God.

God called to the Man: "Where are you?"

He said, "I heard you in the garden and I was afraid because I was naked. And I hid."

God said, "Who told you you were naked? Did you eat from that tree I told you not to eat from?"

The Man said, "The Woman you gave me as a companion, she gave me fruit from the tree, and, yes, I ate it."

God said to the Woman, "What is this that you've done?"

"The serpent seduced me," she said, "and I ate." (Gen. 3:8–13)

what we hear

I'm sure that if the Serpent had had a dog, he would have kicked it. Or at least slapped it with his serpent tail. We've heard it said that people only get married so they'll have someone to blame for things for the rest of their lives. How sad! If you read a little farther in Genesis, you'll see that the consequences of original sin were dire, even beyond separating us from God. The fall meant that *everything* from that moment forward would be difficult. Having children? Painful. Getting a good return for your work? Hard to do. Most days we all feel the direct effects of Adam and Eve's rebellion against God. And it's easy to blame each other. We can imagine that Adam and Eve may have lain awake at night, Eden just a distant memory, and silently blamed each other for the fall. Eve might have thought, *If only Adam had given me the heads-up about that tree … I hadn't even been created yet when God told him about it! If it weren't for Adam, maybe we'd still be in Eden.* Adam might have thought, *Eve looked so good when God first brought her to me, but what a pain she's turned out to be. And eating that fruit! If it hadn't been for her, maybe we'd still be in Eden.* And so it goes. The bitterness comes between us as we participate in a game as old as humanity. It's known as the blame game, and no one ever wins.

what do you hear?

It's not going to do any good to verbalize the stuff you blame your spouse for, but you know what it is. In all these years of blaming him or her for whatever it is, has it changed anything or improved your marriage one iota?

If you have children, you've probably told them on more than one occasion, "You can't blame your brother/sister/friend. You have to take responsibility for your own actions and responses." Do you think *you* do a good job of taking responsibility for your own actions?

Why do you think the blame game has never ceased since the fall of humankind?

extended play

Hold your mate as you pray for him or her. Pray for yourself as well, that God will help you let go of blame and take responsibility for your part in the life you've *both* had a hand in creating—the good and the less-than-good.

twenty five

A Few Choice Words

rhythm

Have a simple picnic in your home, with some fruit and a candle.

listen to the music

A gentle response diffuses anger,
but a sharp tongue kindles a temper-fire.

Kind words heal and help;
cutting words wound and maim. (Prov. 15:1, 4)

Words satisfy the mind as much as fruit does the stomach;
good talk is as gratifying as a good harvest.

Words kill, words give life;
they're either poison or fruit—you choose.

Find a good spouse, you find a good life—
and even more: the favor of God! (Prov. 18:20–22)

Do not let any unwholesome talk come out of your mouths, but
only what is helpful for building others up according to their
needs, that it may benefit those who listen.
(Eph. 4:29 NIV)

A word out of your mouth may seem of no account, but it can accomplish nearly anything—or destroy it!

It only takes a spark, remember, to set off a forest fire. A careless or wrongly placed word out of your mouth can do that. By our speech we can ruin the world, turn harmony to chaos, throw mud on a reputation, send the whole world up in smoke and go up in smoke with it, smoke right from the pit of hell. (James 3:5–6)

what we hear

Fruit or fire? That's the question these Scriptures pose. Which will our words be? As children we would recite the phrase "Sticks and stones may break my bones, but words will never hurt me" in our weak attempt to create a psychological shield against the verbal cruelties that were rampant on the playground. The truth is, sticks and stones may break our bones, but words can reverberate through our minds and spirits long after cuts and bruises are gone. No matter who we are or how tough we may be, at some point in our past, a wounding word was inflicted that took years to overcome. Conversely, some of the words spoken to us have become emotional and spiritual life preservers, keeping us connected to a dream or securing us more closely to our true identity. This is why it's imperative that we, as married lovers, keep a watch over the kinds of words that fill up the air between us. Are we speaking words that are life-giving and affirming ("fruit") or words that are flame throwing and landscape scorching ("fire")? Mangoes or matches? Are you a verbal blesser or a conversational assassin? If you want a strong marriage partner, make sure that your words are building him or her up every day.

what do you hear?

Would you categorize yourself more as a verbal encourager or a verbal flamethrower? Explain.

What "mango" words, if any, have you had for your mate in the past few days?

In what area of your life would you most appreciate hearing a few more mango words from your mate?

extended play

Get literary. Write a mango word of encouragement for your lover and leave it in a place you know he or she will find it. *Bonus:* Your mate can reread your note anytime.

twenty six

Reporting for Duty

rhythm

Do this devo on the floor right *next* to your bed so that you can *discuss* your bed without being *in* it.

listen to the music

It's good for a man to have a wife, and for a woman to have a husband. Sexual drives are strong, but marriage is strong enough to contain them and provide for a balanced and fulfilling sexual life in a world of sexual disorder. The marriage bed must be a place of mutuality—the husband seeking to satisfy his wife, the wife seeking to satisfy her husband. Marriage is not a place to "stand up for your rights." Marriage is a decision to serve the other, whether in bed or out. Abstaining from sex is permissible for a period of time if you both agree to it, and if it's for the purposes of prayer and fasting—but only for such times. Then come back together again. Satan has an ingenious way of tempting us when we least expect it.

(1 Cor. 7:2–5)

what we hear

We know the guys are loving this one! "Honey, you know what Paul wrote: Saying no to sex is OK only if you're praying or fasting." In fact, while we were in the process of writing this book, our church was in the middle of a corporate fast from certain foods and from sex. (We must add that this verse was of little comfort to us at the time!) As husbands and wives, we belong to each other, but Paul tempers that with his reminder in 1 Corinthians 13 that love "does not demand its own way" (v. 5 NLT). The directive of the passage in 1 Corinthians 7 isn't so much a "rule" about having sex (or not) as it is about mutual submission and guarding fidelity. In this spirit, an interruption of the regularity of marital sex ought to be agreed upon and only for spiritual purposes where denial of the flesh is profitable for spiritual empowerment. The word used in the New International Version for "abstaining from sex" is *deprive*, which denotes "robbery" of something that rightfully belongs to your spouse. So have you been a love thief lately? The marriage bed may be a place of "duty," but if only *all* our duties in life were this enjoyable!

what do you hear?

Think about the beds you've slept in during your marriage. Which has been your favorite? Do you like your current bed? Why or why not?

How could you make what goes on between you in your bed a more direct extension of your spiritual life together?

What can you give your lover that you may have been with-holding?

extended play

This might be a great time to think about making your "marriage bed" your favorite place to be. Invest in the best sheets you can afford. Kick the distractions out of the bedroom. Make it a shrine to your love.

Make the bed together—then have fun *un*making it.

twenty seven

Quiver-ing

rhythm

If you have children, camp outside their bedroom door tonight—
quietly!

listen to the music

If God doesn't build the house,
the builders only build shacks.

If God doesn't guard the city,
the night watchman might as well nap.

Don't you see that children are God's best gift?
the fruit of the womb his generous legacy?

Like a warrior's fistful of arrows
are the children of a vigorous youth.

Oh, how blessed are you parents,
with your quivers full of children! (Ps. 127:1, 3–5)

what we hear

Children are a blessing from the Lord. If you have them, you
know this. If you're anticipating them, you'll learn this. If you

can't have them, you know that heartache all too well. We have three children, and we can say that they are, unequivocally, a blessing from God. But children also have the potential to be one of the biggest intimacy killers in your marriage. It's exhausting to parent them, and unfortunately, energy isn't a limitless resource. With the addition of every arrow to your quiver, you have to become more intentional about keeping marital intimacy on the front burner. Interestingly enough, the greatest gift you can give your kids is to have a secure marital love that's firing on all pistons—emotionally, spiritually, physically. Whenever we're involved in PDA (public display of affection), our kids make all sorts of gagging noises and say things like "Get a room" or "I'm throwing up in my own mouth now." But if God blesses us with a long life, we know that our love, which was the genesis of these children, will outlast our roles as parents. And we want to be holding hands in the nursing home. So let the kids make gagging noises. We'll dance to 'em.

what do you hear?

If you have children, can you remember what your life was like before you had them? What, if anything, did you use to do as a couple that you really miss?

How have your children made you two better lovers?

How are you practicing for the empty nest?

extended play

Make yourself an iPod playlist of your favorite get-in-the-mood songs so that you can switch gears between parental-unit mode and remembering-how-we-got-to-be-parental-units mode. If you don't have children, enjoy your nonparental-unit status for as long as it lasts.

twenty eight

Interior Design

rhythm

Park in your driveway where you can look at the outside of your home.

listen to the music

Cultivate inner beauty, the gentle, gracious kind that God delights in. The holy women of old were beautiful before God that way, and were good, loyal wives to their husbands. Sarah, for instance, taking care of Abraham, would address him as "my dear husband." You'll be true daughters of Sarah if you do the same, unanxious and unintimidated.

The same goes for you husbands: Be good husbands to your wives. Honor them, delight in them. As women they lack some of your advantages. But in the new life of God's grace, you're equals. Treat your wives, then, as equals so your prayers don't run aground. (1 Peter 3:4–7)

what we hear

We've seen them before: homes that don't look so great on the outside, but the moment you step inside, you realize that your judgment was premature. The interior of the house—the space where people actually live—is beautiful. The truth is that no one lives across the street from their home (duh). They live on the inside looking out. Whatever people think about your marriage (curb appeal) isn't nearly as important as how you two view each other (interior design). This is why Peter was trying to communicate the truth that it matters how you think about and value your spouse—even how you address him or her! This reveals your interior orientation toward your mate. Do you value your husband's character? Could you call him "my dear husband" and have it ring true? Do you value your wife's character? Can you honestly say to her, "You're my spiritual equal, and your inner beauty captivates me"? These interior designs are the ones that cause a marriage to thrive no matter what the circumstances of life. It takes continual remodeling to make sure that the place where you actually live out your life together exceeds all assumptions—accurate or not—about your marital "curb appeal."

what do you hear?

Do you think that the qualities you're building into the interior of your marriage are causing your marital value to appreciate or depreciate? How so?

Maybe your special names for each other aren't "my dear husband" or "my lovely wife," but you probably have pet names for each other. Do you use these as terms of endearment or as put-downs?

Talk about whether new pet names are in order.

extended play

Tell your mate what parts of his or her character you admire most. If you find it difficult to articulate in the moment, make a date tomorrow to express yourself after you've had time to mull it over.

twenty nine

"Take Two 'Slows' and Call Me in the Morning"

rhythm

If your recliner is big enough—or even if it's not—get into it together with a bowl of ice cream and two spoons.

listen to the music

Post this at all the intersections, dear friends: Lead with your ears, follow up with your tongue, and let anger straggle along in the rear. God's righteousness doesn't grow from human anger. So throw all spoiled virtue and cancerous evil in the garbage. In simple humility, let our gardener, God, landscape you with the Word, making a salvation-garden of your life. (James 1:19–21)

what we hear

Ears are kinda funny looking. If you really start to study them, you can see that some have the little lobes flapping free, some are attached all the way to the bottom, and some have crooked edges. Some people can wiggle their ears; other ears just sit there. (Take a moment to look at your spouse's ears. See? They're funny, no?)

No matter what the shape, ears are designed to receive communication. And James tells us they're the lead players in the pursuit of understanding. This passage is difficult because it flies directly in the face of our normal knee-jerk reaction to conflict. (Notice the word *jerk* plays prominently here.) Our gut reaction is to be quick to speak, quick to anger, and slow to listen. *Au contraire, mon cher!* James's word to us is to flip that script and dial it down. *Way* down. Put the brakes on your first reaction—"Don't bother me with the details"—and switch over to response mode—"Let me hear you out before I cultivate an uninformed emotional freak out." In grade school they used to tell us, "God gave you two ears and one mouth—that should be a clue." Maybe if we put duct tape over our mouths while our partners were speaking, so that we would have to rip it away from our tender skin in order to interrupt or make our point, we might take James's advice a little more to heart.

Honey, where is that roll of that duct tape?

what do you hear?

Is it easier for you to talk or to listen? Why?

What's the difference between *hearing* and *listening?*

Could listening ever be classified as foreplay? (Listen, guys …)

extended play

Listening doesn't always mean the same thing to everyone. Some people prefer active listening in which the hearer actively engages in the conversation, repeating back what was said to make sure the listener understands the speaker before the conversation moves forward. Others just want the hearer to listen silently and not interrupt. Ask your mate how he or she prefers to be listened to. (Don't assume.) Then listen for the answer.

thirty

Marathon Mentality

rhythm

Lace up your sneaks and go walking together. (Bring the book with you.)

listen to the music

Consider it a sheer gift, friends, when tests and challenges come at you from all sides. You know that under pressure, your faith-life is forced into the open and shows its true colors. So don't try to get out of anything prematurely. Let it do its work so you become mature and well-developed, not deficient in any way. If you don't know what you're doing, pray to the Father. He loves to help. You'll get his help, and won't be condescended to when you ask for it. (James 1:2–5)

what we hear

In the world of track and field, certain runners are good at short distances, and others excel in endurance events. When we said "till death do us part" at our wedding, we were committing to a lifetime deal, and even if long distances have never been your emotional forte, baby, you're in it for the long haul now. In a sprint you can see the finish-line tape from the starting line. But marriage isn't like that. We love the words in James, "If you don't know what you're doing, …" Been there, still doing that! We're not sure we've ever had a clue what we've been doing our whole marriage. But we're sure of this: When we said "I do," and the rice was thrown and the honeymoon was over, we were out of the blocks and into a lane built for two in the marriage marathon, with no picture of where the finish line was. Somehow we were supposed to navigate the changes that moved us from being two very distinct entities to becoming "one flesh"—easier said than done. We were one of those couples who got off to a rocky start, but even then we knew that the test wasn't about how we started but about how we'd adapt to the rigors of the road, so we could finish strong. The trials we endure together forge us into a team and actually mature us faster than the periods when we have it easy. We don't have to face the hard times alone, nor do we have to make a go of it with our own wisdom (or lack thereof). All we have to do is ask for what we lack in that department. And James even throws in the bonus of a total absence of condescension in God's generous response. After all, who needs a put-down when you're running for your life? When you're in the middle of a marathon, sometimes all you need is a sign pointing you toward the finish line

what do you hear?
What do you envision your marriage looking like twenty-five years from now?

In what ways have you been guilty of a "sprint mentality" when it comes to your marriage?

What do you think is required to stay in a marriage marathon for the long haul? At what point do you think the "runner's high" might kick in? (*Hint:* Runners say it's right after they've pressed past their "wall"!)

extended play

Race each other back to the house! The winner has to rub the loser's feet—after a shower, of course!

thirty one

High Anxiety

rhythm

Stand in front of your garbage cans, preferably the outside ones. (You know, the ones the trash guys dump once a week.)

listen to the music

Live carefree before God; he is most careful with you. (1 Peter 5:7)

*Cast all your anxiety on him because he cares for you.
(1 Peter 5:7 NIV)*

*Do not be anxious about anything, but in everything, by prayer and petition, with thanksgiving, present your requests to God.
(Phil. 4:6 NIV)*

what we hear

One of you probably gets stressed out because the other one throws stuff away. And one of you probably gets stressed out because the other one won't let you throw stuff away. Same stuff in question, same elevation in blood pressure—totally different reasons. Marriages routinely crumble because of stress. Stress over jobs, finances, commitments, impending decisions. Wouldn't it be nice if we could take that river of stress and divert it before it spills out and overwhelms our spouse? Really, don't we manufacture enough of it on our own without dumping it on the one we love most? The nature of worry and stress is that it has to go somewhere—and Peter tells us that God is in the business of Divine Waste Management. He actually *wants* to take the stress from you. He's rolled the Spiritual Trash Receptacle up to your door and is just waiting for you to throw out the Hefty bag. Your husband or wife was never meant to receive this stress garbage from you. Oh, you might keep it in the kitchen for a day or two, but eventually it starts to smell. And if it piles up over weeks and months, it becomes what health officials call *squalor*—and makes conditions unlivable. This would be the exact opposite of the concept of "carefree," which means we aren't attached to our cares and aren't letting them suck the life out of us. It's just trash. You don't even really want it. So let God have it.

what do you hear?

What is registering on your High Anxiety Scale this week? How is this stress affecting your relationship with your spouse?

Are you really convinced that you're better able to handle this than God? Or are you afraid he might not have your back this time?

In what ways could you build more "tossing out" into your marriage?

extended play

Maybe it's a good time to throw out some spiritual garbage—
and some material garbage as well. It's great to let go of things.
On the FlyLady.net Web site, the author advises throwing out
twenty-seven unused items per week, just to get in the habit of
regularly letting go of things. (They don't have to be big
things—maybe just twenty worn-out rubber bands and three
chewed-up Frisbees and four expired coupons.) You can donate
your stuff to charity, share it with someone who needs it, or literally just throw it away.

thirty two

The Best for Last

rhythm

Relax in your rocking chairs. What, you don't have any? You're missing so much if you don't—specifically, practice for old age.

listen to the music

And the master of the banquet tasted the water that had been turned into wine. He did not realize where it had come from, though the servants who had drawn the water knew. Then he called the bridegroom aside and said, "Everyone brings out the choice wine first and then the cheaper wine after the guests have had too much to drink; but you have saved the best till now." (John 2:9–10 NIV)

what we hear

Isn't it great that Jesus performed his first miracle at a wedding? His mother got a little pushy with him, but he saved the evening and even went above and beyond to make the finish unexpectedly spectacular. We think he's been performing miracles at weddings ever since—taking two people with pushy mothers and starting them on a path to something sweeter and more intoxicating with time.

When couples are early in their love relationship, they think it's the best it will ever be. But the definite upside of a long-term committed marriage is the fact that if the connection is ever-strengthening, ever-growing, the best and the sweetest is yet to come (even to outside observers).

At the conclusion of every service in our church, our pastor has us tell each other, "Your best and brightest days are still ahead of you." As believers, we know this to be a spiritual certainty because of God's presence in our lives and the promise of heaven. But Robert Browning was onto something regarding married love when he penned the words "Grow old along with me! / The best is yet to be." It's the mark of youth to begin with excitement. It's the gift of age to richly appreciate the best that only time can bestow.

what do you hear?

Talk about the ways in which your love is richer than it was the day you said "I do."

What are some of the surprises that time has revealed about your mate?

Do you think you two will be the hottest couple in the nursing home? If not, get yourselves pointed in that direction!

extended play

We don't think there's an age limit for parking (and we're not talking "parallel"). Consider taking it up again.

thirty three

Timing Is Everything

rhythm

Sit someplace where you can watch the world coming and going—maybe looking out on your street, where people in different life stages are passing by.

listen to the music

There is a time for everything,

and a season for every activity under heaven:

a time to be born and a time to die,

a time to plant and a time to uproot,

a time to kill and a time to heal,

a time to tear down and a time to build,

a time to weep and a time to laugh,

a time to mourn and a time to dance,

a time to scatter stones and a time to gather them,

a time to embrace and a time to refrain,

a time to search and a time to give up,

a time to keep and a time to throw away,

a time to tear and a time to mend,

a time to be silent and a time to speak,

a time to love and a time to hate,

a time for war and a time for peace. (Eccl. 3:1–8 NIV)

what we hear

Wasn't it Dr. John who sang "I been in the right place, but it must have been the wrong time"? Raise your hand if you know what he's talking about. If it weren't for the timing issue, we conjecture that fully half of our communication breakdowns would be remedied. But it just so happens that the very moment you really *need* to communicate something important to your spouse, he or she is usually in no frame of mind to receive it. Or if you two don't have a designated time for an informational/emotional download during the day, then you're likely to be constantly throwing out info on the fly, never really knowing if you've been heard. This leaves you feeling somewhat rejected and unimportant, neither of which are probably true, but in that moment, it *feels* true.

So how do you remedy this ever-present problem? One way is to be a great observer of your mate. Do you have a handle on his or her daily rhythms, stressors, good times? A particular time when you know your lover is more receptive? Do you have a stack of Post-it Notes so you can hold on to important communication until the moment is opportune? Timing is (almost) everything.

what do you hear?

Relate a time in the past couple of weeks when your partner told you something and the timing was just atrocious. Why do you think the timing mattered?

Do you have a time of day that's pretty much always a bad time for your spouse to try to talk with you? Can you both agree to respect each other's timing preferences?

Which of you is the better discussion deferrer? Why? (*Hint:* Does one of you fear that a discussion delay means that the issue won't get discussed at all?)

extended play

Planned time for each other must be paramount, especially if you have kids. Set aside regular times to hear one another and *never* break dates with each other.

thirty four

The Love SAT

rhythm

Grab a pencil and some paper. There's a short essay test at the end.

listen to the music

If I speak with human eloquence and angelic ecstasy but don't love, I'm nothing but the creaking of a rusty gate.

If I speak God's Word with power, revealing all his mysteries and making everything plain as day, and if I have faith that says to a mountain, "Jump," and it jumps, but I don't love, I'm nothing.

If I give everything I own to the poor and even go to the stake to be burned as a martyr, but I don't love, I've gotten nowhere. So, no matter what I say, what I believe, and what I do, I'm bankrupt without love.

Love never gives up.

Love cares more for others than for self.

Love doesn't want what it doesn't have.

Love doesn't strut,

Doesn't have a swelled head,

Doesn't force itself on others,

Isn't always "me first,"

Doesn't fly off the handle,
Doesn't keep score of the sins of others,
Doesn't revel when others grovel,
Takes pleasure in the flowering of truth,
Puts up with anything,
Trusts God always,
Always looks for the best,
Never looks back,
But keeps going to the end.
Love never dies. (1 Cor. 13:1–8)

what we hear

We realize the kind of love described in this passage is a very tall order. It's like continually attempting to get a higher score on a standardized exam, knowing you'll probably *never* get 100 percent. But every year you try to up your marks.

One time we were on a long flight the weekend before Valentine's Day, and the airline had chosen *Love Story* as the in-flight movie. We watched with our headsets on and tried not to laugh out loud when the most famous line of that movie was delivered: "Love means never having to say you're sorry." It's not that it's funny per se; it's just that it's a highly idealized view of love that has absolutely *nothing* to do with the real world. You know, the world where both of us routinely mess up, and we're forced to choose which tack we'll take: admitting our mistake and finding the humility to ask forgiveness; or just playing it like nothing ever happened and hoping it'll go away. The thirteenth chapter of 1 Corinthians has been dubbed the "Love Chapter" because it equates love with a specific set of attributes and actions including: perseverance, humility, gentleness, and a commitment to truth. Here we learn that love means you not only routinely have to say you're sorry, but you also have to receive an apology with a gracious spirit when your spouse says it to you. As the apostle Peter reminds us, "Most of all, love each other as if your life depended on it. Love makes up for practically anything" (1 Peter 4:8).

what do you hear?

Does one of you have the "Fonzie Problem"? (The Fonz on the TV show *Happy Days* was physically unable to say the words "I was w-w-w-w-w-w-wrong.")

What if your life depended on the level of love you show on a daily basis? How long do you think you'd survive?

Would you say that most of the time your first reaction to a difficult interpersonal situation is love? How, specifically, did you express a 1 Corinthians–type of love during a recent time of stress?

extended play

Paraphrase 1 Corinthians 13 in terms that apply to your marriage. Make it personal. (For example: "If I give my body to yard work and understand all bank statements but have no love, I am zip, zero, nada …")

thirty five

Your In-Laws Just Might Know a Thing or Two

rhythm

Go to the place where one of you burns the midnight oil in your household.

listen to the music

Story setup: Moses was working too hard, trying to do it all himself. His father-in-law observed it. Pick up story line:

> Moses' father-in-law said, "This is no way to go about [judging disputes]. You'll burn out, and the people right along with you. This is way too much for you—you can't do this alone. Now listen to me. Let me tell you how to do this so that God will be in this with you. Be there for the people before God, but let the matters of concern be presented to God. Your job is to teach them the rules and instructions, to show them how to live, what to do. And then you need to keep a sharp eye out for competent men.
>
> Moses listened to the counsel of his father-in-law and did everything he said.

Then Moses said good-bye to his father-in-law who went home to his own country. (Ex. 18:17–21, 24, 27)

what we hear

We've heard it said that if you look up in the family tree far enough, you'll probably find squirrels. It's easy to dismiss your in-laws as nosy people who are trying to tell you how to run your life, when, in reality, they probably just want the best for you and your marriage and may have an issue or two with boundaries or personal space. But every once in a while, your in-laws might just have some wisdom you truly need. Such was the case with Moses. His father-in-law gave him the first management-training course, which amounted to this: "Moses, Moses … You're wearing yourself out and neglecting my daughter. Dude, you have to delegate." But that's not the most amazing thing about this passage. The great thing is that Moses actually listened to his father-in-law's counsel and "did everything he said." Moses didn't let his ego or his pride keep him from hearing a necessary truth from his wife's dad.

Your in-laws (on either side) may be a little crazy, but sometimes those crazy people know a thing or two. Be humble enough to love and listen to your mate's parents. Of course, maybe *the* most amazing thing in the Moses story is that the father-in-law knew when to go back home.

what do you hear?

Name one attribute you truly admire about your in-laws. (Come on; it's just one! You can come up with *one*.)

Describe a time, if any, when you received insight from your in-laws that unlocked a key piece of your mate's history and really helped you better understand him or her.

How would you describe your relationship with your in-laws? How does this affect your marriage (for better or worse)?

extended play

This may be a stretch for some of you, but try to write a short note or make a phone call to your in-laws to let them know how much you appreciate them for raising a person who knew a good thing when he or she saw it … and married you!

thirty six

Giving What You Want

rhythm

Go to the kitchen and grab two forks. Then park yourselves somewhere near the fridge.

listen to the music

Don't pick on people, jump on their failures, criticize their faults—unless, of course, you want the same treatment. Don't condemn those who are down; that hardness can boomerang. Be easy on people; you'll find life a lot easier. Give away your life; you'll find life given back, but not merely given back—given back with bonus and blessing. Giving, not getting, is the way. Generosity begets generosity. (Luke 6:37–38)

what we hear

It's a common theme in marital counseling: "How am I supposed to function when my spouse won't give me what I *need?*" The question is the off-ramp into a predictable downward spiral: The wife says, "I won't give him what he needs because he's not giving me what I need!" to which the husband replies, "Well, I won't give her what she needs because she's not giving me what I need!" You get the picture. The Golden Rule states, "Do unto others as you would have them do unto you." We seem to *think* it says, "Do unto others once they've done unto you the thing you'd like to have done unto you." But it's just not gonna happen.

We once heard an allegory about mealtime in heaven and hell. It turns out that in both places, meals are served at a huge round table with lots of delicious food in the center. The food is out of reach, but everyone has forks with long handles. In hell, everyone starves because even though people can reach the food with their forks, the forks are too long to bring the food back to their mouths. In heaven, faced with the same problem, people eat just fine. How? By taking the food on their forks and feeding it to those across from them. Same problem, vastly different solution. It seems counterintuitive to our lesser nature, but Jesus taught us that the kingdom of heaven is upside down. Do you want to lead? Serve. Do you want to be first? Be last. Do you want to live? Die to yourself. Whatever you need, give it.

what do you hear?

What one thing do you think you really need to get from your spouse?

How can you give that thing in a tangible way?

Discuss a time when the kingdom-upside-down principle was evident in your marriage.

extended play

Maybe your wedding cake was the last thing you fed each other. Find something in the fridge that you can feed to your mate. It's good practice for old age!

thirty seven

Standard-Issue Uniform

rhythm

Meet in the laundry room. If you can sit on the washer or dryer, all the better.

listen to the music

So, chosen by God for this new life of love, dress in the wardrobe God picked out for you: compassion, kindness, humility, quiet strength, discipline. Be even-tempered, content with second place, quick to forgive an offense. Forgive as quickly and completely as the Master forgave you. And regardless of what else you put on, wear love. It's your basic, all-purpose garment. Never be without it. (Col. 3:12–14)

what we hear

The scene is so universal, it's almost cliché. A woman is standing in her closet saying, "I have absolutely nothing to wear." And her husband is singing to himself (in his best KC and the Sunshine Band impersonation), "That's the way—uh-huh, uh-huh—I like it—uh-huh, uh-huh." But men don't understand that women get dressed the same way they do practically everything else—*emotionally*. What she really means when she says she doesn't have anything to wear is: "I don't have anything I *feel* like wearing." It has very little to do with the temperature outside or her plans for the day; it has everything to do with whether she "feels" like wearing blue or red, tailored or spandex (aka, "I feel fat today").

This will forever be a mystery to men, because they never "feel" *any* way about their clothing choice for the day. If it *smells* clean and is remotely connected to this decade, it's a good choice. Paul tells us that no matter what we put on spiritually, the proper topper (and "foundation garment," for that matter) is *love*. It's to be our underlying motive for everything we do and the topcoat that covers over and protects us from becoming cranky and easily offended. Love for women it's the perfect pair of black shoes; for men it's the comfortable pair of khaki slacks—is the basic necessity of your spiritual wardrobe.

what do you hear?

If your wardrobe reflected your spiritual life, what would you be wearing?

Are you a quick forgiver, or do you hold on to your forgiveness like a bargaining chip?

How can you help each other dress for success spiritually?

extended play

Try this next time you have a night out: Let your mate choose your outfit. Even if it's not your favorite, wear it! You might even be surprised to find out what kind of clothing your spouse enjoys seeing you wear.

thirty eight

Marks-a-Lot

rhythm

Sit or stand in front of where you keep your family pictures.

listen to the music

"Each of you heft a stone to your shoulder, a stone for each of the tribes of the People of Israel, so you'll have something later to mark the occasion. When your children ask you, 'What are these stones to you?' you'll say, 'The flow of the Jordan was stopped in front of the Chest of the Covenant of God as it crossed the Jordan—stopped in its tracks. These stones are a permanent memorial for the People of Israel.'"

Joshua set up the twelve stones taken from the middle of the Jordan that had marked the place where the priests who carried the Chest of the Covenant had stood. They are still there today. (Josh. 4:6–7, 9)

what we hear

Memory is a tricky thing. It starts out like superglue, turns into Elmer's along the way, morphs into Post-it Notes, and eventually ends up like Teflon. Whether you're young or old or in between, it's easy to forget. The young forget because they're too busy going and doing. The old forget because they've put so many pieces of information into their brains that their internal memory chips are overloaded with megabytes of people and places and events. Whatever the reason, it seems we all benefit from some visual cues to help us remember whatever is important to us.

Joshua knew this tendency we have to forget God's goodness and provision in our lives. If we don't mark the important events, we can lose our connection to both the event and how we felt about it at the time. Markers give us an opportunity to speak to the next generation about the times when God has been faithful to us. We built a rock waterfall in our backyard the year there was a significant shift in our life and ministry. It has become a tangible reminder of how our faith was tested that year and how God never let us down. In Joshua's day it was a pile of rocks. In your marriage it may be a bucket of seashells, a painting that commemorates a special event, or just some trinkets or scraps of paper in a memento box. The simplest items can memorialize shared miracles, answered prayers, and significant moments in a marriage while serving as a visual story line of your union with each other before God.

what do you hear?

What are some of the meaningful markers in your marriage? (Maybe you didn't recognize them as such at the time, but almost everyone has them.)

How can you display these items so they can spark meaningful conversation with each other and your family?

How could the stories behind these markers become part of the legacy of your union? What events would you most want to share with your grandchildren someday?

extended play

Agree on a recent event in your married life that deserves to be memorialized. Decide on an appropriate marker—then mark it well.

thirty nine

The Hulk Effect

rhythm

Hang out wherever there's some exercise equipment—in the basement, at the gym.

listen to the music

Jacob set out again on his way to the people of the east. He noticed a well out in an open field with three flocks of sheep bedded down around it. This was the common well from which the flocks were watered. The stone over the mouth of the well was huge. When all the flocks were gathered, the shepherds would roll the stone from the well and water the sheep; then they would return the stone, covering the well.

Jacob said, "There's a lot of daylight still left; it isn't time to round up the sheep yet, is it? So why not water the flocks and go back to grazing?"

"We can't," they said. "Not until all the shepherds get here. It takes all of us to roll the stone from the well. Not until then can we water the flocks."

While Jacob was in conversation with them, Rachel came up with her father's sheep. She was the shepherd. The moment Jacob

*spotted Rachel, daughter of Laban his mother's brother, saw her
arriving with his uncle Laban's sheep, he went and single-handedly
rolled the stone from the mouth of the well and watered the sheep of
his uncle Laban. (Gen. 29:1–3, 7–10)*

what we hear

The Hulk, Conan the Barbarian, King Kong—it's all the same. See girl, move something big. What can we say? Love makes you do crazy things. We make outrageous statements like "I would climb the highest mountain, swim the deepest ocean—whatever it takes to win your love!" This is the stuff great love songs are made of. There's some sort of innate power in that first blast of "I've got that lovin' feeling" that inspires feats of greatness in men. Then somehow it devolves from "I can single-handedly move this boulder!" to "This trash bag must be kryptonite." The trick is to tap into that early sense of inspiration for the long haul—to constantly be striving to impress your lover on continuously evolving planes. You might not be able to move a boulder anymore, but your strength of character can be flexed almost anytime. The feats become more internal; the payoff, more long lasting.

what do you hear?

Can you remember something one of you did early in your relationship to impress the other? Does it seem silly to you now? Did it seem crazy then?

What are some internal character qualities that continue to impress you as you observe your partner?

Tell each other about something positive the other has done recently that totally surprised you—you know, really took you off guard!

extended play

Hold each other's feet for a few sit-ups. (Who can do the most?) It can be more fun to work out together a few times a week than it is alone. And remember that lovemaking has excellent cardio-vascular benefits.

forty

Hope Floats

rhythm

Got a fishin' pole with a bobber? Get it out and stick it in some water—even if it's just the bathtub.

listen to the music

We rejoice in the hope of the glory of God. Not only so, but we also rejoice in our sufferings, because we know that suffering produces perseverance; perseverance, character; and character, hope. And hope does not disappoint us, because God has poured out his love into our hearts by the Holy Spirit, whom he has given us. (Rom. 5:2–5 NIV)

"For I know the plans I have for you," declares the Lord, "plans to prosper you and not to harm you, plans to give you hope and a future." (Jer. 29:11 NIV)

And we know that in all things God works for the good of those who love him, who have been called according to his purpose. (Rom. 8:28 NIV)

what we hear

Hope is a buoyant thing. It bobbles up on top of the water no matter how rough that water becomes. It just keeps rising to the top—perhaps temporarily washed over, but never sunk. But hope is only as good as its source, so thank God, it's not us. For those of us who have placed our faith in God, we're assured that hope is forever.

The Scriptures in the previous section don't sugarcoat the truth that life will be very, very hard sometimes. During those times our faith is put to the test, and we're given the chance to see exactly how far the boundaries of our faith extend. We don't know who among us could say, like Job, "Though he slay me, yet will I hope in him" (Job 13:15 NIV). Suffering is part and parcel of life here on earth. But for believers, it yields perseverance, character, and hope. Whenever we have no idea what the plan is, we still know that God has one. And even though we can't see the good in a particular circumstance, we can have a quiet assurance that God is somehow working his way toward a good outcome. In our human unions, hope is the commodity that must never be simultaneously lost by both companions. In our marriage we have this rule: Only one of us is allowed to be depressed at a time. We just have to take turns, because one of us must be in charge of saying, "God has never forsaken us yet. You may not be able to see the buoy right now, but I can."

what do you hear?

Talk about a time during your years together when all hope seemed lost.

Is there a situation in your marriage history when you couldn't see how it could ever be turned into something good, yet it was?

Which of you is naturally more optimistic than the other?

extended play
Take your honey fishin'—who cares if you catch anything?

interlude two

Total Communion

One of the most intimate things we can do together as couples is to establish spiritual rituals. The very fact that you are reading this book says that you're involved in a quest to enrich your life of faith and love together. Reading Scripture together, talking about it, and praying together will serve to strengthen your bond and draw you closer to God.

It's wonderful when we, with our church family, partake in a Communion service. We feel at once drawn closer to Christ and to his body. In the same way, you may find that you want to increase your spiritual bonding by practicing the sacrament of Holy Communion together as husband and wife. There's a certain intimacy in celebrating the very core of our faith, Christ's sacrifice for our atonement, that can cause us to reflect on our lives and commit to loving each other more sacrificially, as Christ has loved and given himself for us.

When you feel ready to establish this practice in your own home, we offer this guide (adapted from our church's Communion guide for husbands and wives) as a suggested outline for your time together. This is only a guide. You may also want to watch the movie *The Passion of the Christ* together as a way to help you focus on Christ's ultimate sacrifice and prepare your hearts to commemorate his love for you.

preparation

Assemble two glasses, some grape juice or wine (depending on your church practice), and some type of bread that doesn't contain yeast (a flatbread or cracker is fine). These are symbolic elements, so don't get hung up on it all being perfect; it's more important that you focus on the meaning behind the symbols.

Find a quiet place in your home where you'll be free from distractions. Unplug the phone. Light a candle. Draw close to each other. Open your Bible to 1 Corinthians 11:23–26. We ask that the husband take this opportunity to be "a priest of his home" and lead in the observance.

the observance

Pray together: "Lord, we ask that this time of Communion will lead us to greater intimacy with Christ and with each other."

Read Isaiah 53:4–6:

But the fact is, it was our pains he carried—
  our disfigurements, all the things wrong with us.
We thought he brought it on himself,
  that God was punishing him for his own failures.
But it was our sins that did that to him,
  that ripped and tore and crushed him—our sins!
He took the punishment, and that made us whole.
  Through his bruises we get healed.
We're all like sheep who've wandered off and gotten lost.
  We've all done our own thing, gone our own way.
And God has piled all our sins, everything we've done wrong,
  on him, on him.

Ask yourselves these questions: Before we take Communion together, is there any issue, problem, concern, or sin that would affect the purity of this time together? Are our minds and hearts clean to continue?

After preparing your hearts, read aloud the following passage from 1 Corinthians 11:23–26 (NIV), beginning with the element representing Christ's body (the bread): "For I received from the Lord what I also passed on to you: The Lord Jesus, on the night he was betrayed, took bread, and when he had given thanks, he broke it and said, 'This is my body, which is for you; do this in remembrance of me.'"

Eat the bread together.

Then pour the element representing the blood of Jesus into the glasses. Husbands, give a glass to your wife, and hold your glasses while you (the husband) read verse 25: "In the same way, after supper he took the cup, saying, 'This cup is the new covenant in my blood; do this, whenever you drink it, in remembrance of me.'"

Drink together.

Read verse 26: "For whenever you eat this bread and drink this cup, you proclaim the Lord's death until he comes"

Reflect and pray silently for a few moments, giving thanks for the sacrifice Jesus made, so that we can be heirs of salvation together under the grace of God.

Pray together: "Lord, thank you for your sacrifice and your extreme love for us. Thank you for this time together. Thank you for calling us to love you and to love each other. May your sacrifice teach us how to love sacrificially. God, keep us close to you and close to each other."

forty one

Hurry Home

rhythm

Head straight to your home's entryway or foyer—do not pass go.

listen to the music

Restless in bed and sleepless through the night, I longed for my lover.
I wanted him desperately. His absence was painful.

So I got up, went out and roved the city,
hunting through streets and down alleys.

I wanted my lover in the worst way!
I looked high and low, and didn't find him.

And then the night watchmen found me
as they patrolled the darkened city.
"Have you seen my dear lost love?" I asked.

No sooner had I left them than I found him,
found my dear lost love.

I threw my arms around him and held him tight,
wouldn't let him go until I had him home again,
safe at home beside the fire. (Song 3:1–4)

Run to me, dear lover.
  Come like a gazelle,

Leap like a wild stag
  on the spice mountains. (Song 8:14)

what we hear

Where is your favorite place? Is it in some far-flung country across the sea? Is it an exciting locale in another state? If you're like us, it's about twelve inches inside your front door. Be it ever so humble, home is a haven, a refuge, a soft place to land. For most of us, home is where we feel safest. It can also be the place where we're desired, the place where our wildest dreams can come true, the place of our highest fulfillment and greatest passion—*if* we aren't so weary of the world that we can't find energy to show our lover the passion he or she deserves. In Solomon's song, the woman actually goes out looking to bring her man back home, and she won't rest until he's physically present.

When you think of home, does your heart skip a beat? Do your thoughts turn to memories of intimacy with your spouse? Do you miss each other the moment you part and think of the moment you'll be together again? Or when you think of home, does a never-ending list of chores and repairs and expenses come to mind? Home isn't an address on a mailbox but a pair of waiting arms.

what do you hear?

What aspects of home mean the most to you? What do you and your partner do to make your home a place of intimacy and connection?

When you're driving home from wherever your day takes you, do you long for the moment your feet get inside your own front door? Why or why not?

When you think of home, what particular spot comes to mind? Kitchen table? Recliner? Bed? Backyard?

extended play

Have a date at home. If you have kids, get a sitter to take them off-site and enjoy having the place all to yourselves.

forty two

Bring It On

rhythm
Go to wherever the husband's most prized material possession is kept.

listen to the music

What's this I see, approaching from the desert,
  raising clouds of dust,

Filling the air with sweet smells
  and pungent aromatics?

Look! It's Solomon's carriage,
  carried and guarded by sixty soldiers,
  sixty of Israel's finest,

All of them armed to the teeth,
  trained for battle,
  ready for anything, anytime.

King Solomon once had a carriage built
  from fine-grained Lebanon cedar.

He had it framed with silver and roofed with gold.
  The cushions were covered with a purple fabric,
  the interior lined with tooled leather.

Come and look, sisters in Jerusalem.
   Oh, sisters of Zion, don't miss this!

My King-Lover,
   dressed and garlanded for his wedding,
   his heart full, bursting with joy! (Song 3:6–11)

what we hear

It's not easy to be Clark Kent all the time, especially when you know you're capable of so much more. An innate need is encoded into the DNA of the male species to occasionally make a grand gesture that elicits a grand response from his lover. Solomon, who up until this point has been the gentle, flirting wooer, suddenly brings out the peacock feathers of his full kingly privileges and makes his statement. He's looking g-o-o-d. He's kicking up dust from quite a ways away, and it's pretty impressive. And does his beloved ever respond! Without the gesture, there would have been nothing for her to comment on. Without her comment, his gesture would have been wasted. It's a delicate emotional dance rooted not just in ego fulfillment but in the show of strength that makes him primary in her sight and lets her know that there's an element of security in his strength. This kind of display isn't necessary every day, but it's nice to trot it out every once in a while.

what do you hear?

Guys, do you have an inexplicable urge to just show off every now and then for your woman?

What's different in the way you did it before you were married and the way you do it now?

How does it make you feel when your woman takes notice and responds with admiration?

extended play

OK, ladies—even if you can't understand why your man needs to watch testosterone-driven shoot-'em-up movies, agree to go to one for every chick flick you make him see with you.

forty three

Frequent Pit Stops

rhythm

Go to your car together and sit in the front seats.

listen to the music

Love from the center of who you are; don't fake it. Run for dear life from evil; hold on for dear life to good. Be good friends who love deeply; practice playing second fiddle.

Don't burn out; keep yourselves fueled and aflame.

(Rom. 12:9–11)

what we hear

Anyone familiar with NASCAR knows that without well-timed pit stops, the race is lost, no matter how talented the driver. No fuel equals no finish. That's why it's essential that you schedule time in your marriage for periodic intensive reconnection that you just can't fit in on every single lap. The first part of the Romans passage discusses the integrity of the vehicle (using authentic engine parts). God made you to be uniquely you. He made your spouse to be uniquely himself or herself. If either of you is trying to be someone other than who you are, you're literally wasting your time here on earth. God called each of you into a relationship with each other to become more than either of you could become alone.

This passage also speaks of embracing good in your life (tires that grip the road) and being "good friends." The truth is that because we're lovers, we have the unique ability to be friends who know and accept each other on the most intimate level. We have the inside track, and with that comes the responsibility to help each other stay fueled for the journey.

Finally, Romans also highlights the willingness to take the lesser slot for the good of the team. (In car racing this is called "draft position.") At different times in your marriage, one of you will need to take the draft position to create the elements necessary for a "win" for your spouse. When one of you wins, the marriage wins. The team wins. And, as all good NASCAR fans know, when you're in the winner's circle, don't forget to thank your sponsors.

what do you hear?

In different categories of your life (personally, professionally, spiritually, relationally), do you feel like you're at the beginning of your race, somewhere in the middle, or coming into the home stretch? Explain.

Your marriage "vehicle" will always need to make a pit stop from time to time to keep it well fueled and well treaded. What activities could you put on the calendar as relationship pit stops? A quiet retreat? A trip where you put some large-scale questions on the table and pray about your lives? A couples' retreat or conference?

When was the last time you, as a couple, intentionally rested together?

extended play
Do some research on the concept of Sabbath (the biblical mandate of taking one day a week for rest and rejuvenation). What are some ways to incorporate this God-ordained practice into your marriage?

forty four

A Sacred Trust

rhythm

Sit on the floor cross-legged, knees touching. If you aren't flexible enough to achieve this, have fun trying.

listen to the music

Honor marriage, and guard the sacredness of sexual intimacy between wife and husband. God draws a firm line against casual and illicit sex.

Don't be obsessed with getting more material things. Be relaxed with what you have. Since God assured us, "I'll never let you down, never walk off and leave you," we can boldly quote,
God is there, ready to help;
I'm fearless no matter what.
Who or what can get to me? (Heb. 13:4–6)

what we hear

Trust is an elusive concept. We talk about it and say we value it, but if you ask someone to define it, the words are hard to find. However, we definitely know when it has been broken. It's interesting that the writer of Hebrews links a fear of abandonment and the desire for more material things to the instruction to guard your marriage, as these things don't seem related at first glance. But why would we be tempted to stray in the first place, unless we *wanted more* and *felt alone?*

When someone is headed to the outer edges of his or her marital vows, that person will invariably confide to the new love interest, "I feel so alone. I just know I want more in a relationship." In the movie *Meet the Parents,* there's a running joke about the familial "circle of trust." Either you're on the inside or the outside—there's nothing in between. No circle is tighter than the bonds of a sworn promise made between a husband and wife. That circle of trust is sacred. It's completely closed and should be so emotionally and physically. This is why Jesus told the Pharisees that *committing* adultery isn't the only sin; the mere *contemplation* of it is just as sinful. The act and the thought are one and the same. Jesus knew the truth: The intent of the heart is at the root of the faithfulness issue.

Some houses have picket fences (cute for decoration), some have chain-link fences (good for keeping things in), and others have concrete walls (perfect for keeping things out). Make sure you're building your marital fences out of the right material.

what do you hear?

Identify any weak areas in your marital circle of trust. Is anyone lurking around the edges, posing some kind of threat (friends, family members, business associates)?

Would you classify yourself as "generally content" or "always looking for a little bit more"? How does this attitude affect you spiritually?

Do you have a problem trusting people? Is there something in your past that makes trust difficult for you now? Talk about it.

extended play

In the corporate world, companies have entire weekends devoted to trust-building exercises. What trust-building exercises could you do as a couple?

forty five

Bill of Rights

rhythm
Sit on some steps—inside or outside. Try to fit on the same one.

listen to the music
If you've gotten anything at all out of following Christ, if his love has made any difference in your life, if being in a community of the Spirit means anything to you, if you have a heart, if you care—then do me a favor: Agree with each other, love each other, be deep-spirited friends. Don't push your way to the front; don't sweet-talk your way to the top. Put yourself aside, and help others get ahead. Don't be obsessed with getting your own advantage. Forget yourselves long enough to lend a helping hand.

Think of yourselves the way Christ Jesus thought of himself. He had equal status with God but didn't think so much of himself that he had to cling to the advantages of that status no matter what. (Phil. 2:1–5)

what we hear
TV psychologist Dr. Phil is fond of saying, "So do you want to be right or do you want to be happy?" Another of his go-to sayings is, "And how is that working for you?"

There's usually at least one partner in a marriage whose job it is to defend his or her rightness at all costs. That spouse will do this even to his or her own detriment—as if the rightness justifies the meanness or coldness. The apostle Paul tells us that rightness doesn't necessarily equal happiness. So you're right; so what? How's that working for you? Making things sweeter between you two? Leading to closeness and intimacy? Or is defending "the principle" (whatever *that* means) pushing your mate aside?

It takes a good dose of humility to let go of the need to always be "right" and not do it with a condescending look. But every time you do, you're actually emulating Christ rather than clinging to the advantage of your rightness. Jesus let go of his divine rights in order to come to us and give us God's love in human form. Don't just do Paul a favor; do yourselves a favor: "Agree with each other, love each other, be deep-spirited friends." And remember, the next time you're standing on "principle," you might just be standing on the lesser one.

what do you hear?

Recall a time, if any, when you were definitely in the right, but it turned out to be oh so wrong. (*General principle:* If you find yourself searching Google more than once a day to prove a point, you might be addicted to your own rightness.)

Which is the higher priority for you personally—being right or having peace in your relationship?

When you finally prove your point and you actually *are* right, how do you think it makes your mate feel?

extended play

Practice being wrong at least once a week just to stay in shape. (OK, so it's more like *admit* being wrong at least once a week, because all of us are wrong at least that often.)

forty six

Improving on Perfection

rhythm

Does one of you play a musical instrument? Get it out and play it for your partner—kazoos and paper on combs are legitimate, too.

listen to the music

My beloved friends, let us continue to love each other since love comes from God. Everyone who loves is born of God and experiences a relationship with God. The person who refuses to love doesn't know the first thing about God, because God is love—so you can't know him if you don't love. This is how God showed his love for us: God sent his only Son into the world so we might live through him. This is the kind of love we are talking about not that we once upon a time loved God, but that he loved us and sent his Son as a sacrifice to clear away our sins and the damage they've done to our relationship with God.

My dear, dear friends, if God loved us like this, we certainly ought to love each other. No one has seen God, ever. But if we love one another, God dwells deeply within us, and his love becomes complete in us—perfect love! (1 John 4:7–12)

what we hear

We all occasionally have moments when everything feels almost perfect, but unadulterated perfection is hard to find. It's impossible to find in human beings. Despite what your mama may have told you, none of us is a bargain. We're all flawed, scarred, and broken. We come to marriage bruised by life, tattered around the edges, and incomplete. As Rocky Balboa explained to Adrian's brother (when asked what Rocky saw in his sister), "I dunno, she's got gaps, I got gaps, together we fill gaps." That's at least part of what we are to each other—carpenter's putty. Or at least that's what we should be.

Some people use their knowledge of their spouse's gaps to ridicule and belittle them. Their intimate knowledge of the gaps becomes their weapon of choice. But John tells us that God's love in our relationships turns that tendency on its head. Knowing each other's gaps should lead to tender mercy and sacrifice, giving us the opportunity to love as God has loved us. Rocky's "Gap Theory" is almost right—and we know the rest of the story: God's love fills the gaps between us better than we ever could.

what do you hear?

Relate to your mate one of the gaps he or she fills in your life.

How does God's love operating in your life increase your capacity to love your spouse?

Why does loving each other sometimes feel like the least you can do, and at other times feel like the most you can do?

extended play

Based on the knowledge you have of your mate now, how would you propose if you could do it all over again? (This is for both or you, not just the one who proposed!)

forty seven

Carpe Diem, Y'all

rhythm

Meet up in the basement, game room, or playroom.

listen to the music

Seize life! Eat bread with gusto,

Drink wine with a robust heart.

Oh yes—God takes pleasure in your pleasure!

Dress festively every morning.

Don't skimp on colors and scarves.

Relish life with the spouse you love

Each and every day of your precarious life.

Each day is God's gift. It's all you get in exchange

For the hard work of staying alive.

Make the most of each one!

Whatever turns up, grab it and do it. And heartily!
   (Eccl. 9:7–10)

what we hear

We've heard it said that it's not so much about having the "time of your life" as it is about having "more life in your time." We've all known people who are afraid to live fully because they live cautiously, erring more on the side of fear than of faith. You can be eighty years old chronologically and yet have truly lived only fifteen years because you spent sixty-five years fearing death. Conversely, some people leave this earth at a relatively young age but have lived all their years to the fullest.

The writer of Ecclesiastes tells us that we have a responsibility to embrace our days with gusto—not in the beer-commercial, "You only go around once" way, but in the "God's love makes me fearless" way. You can spend your days stuck in the emotional prisons of your past or worried to the point of paralysis about the future. Neither of these stances satisfies a heart that longs to be present to the gifts God brings you every day. You're to "relish life with the spouse you love." That's a biblical directive! If you're just existing with the spouse you love or barely making it with the spouse you love, you're not living up to your love potential, my friend. A colorful life is a loving gift you give your family and yourself. Go for it! And do it heartily!

what do you hear?

What parts of your marriage are already pretty colorful and full of pleasure?

What areas of your marriage could stand a little more color?

Who do you think of as someone who packs a lot of life in his or her time?

extended play

Talk about the most romantic twenty-four hours you've ever had together. Now plan another twenty-four to top them. Seize the day!

forty eight

Grab Your Spurs!

rhythm

Go to the westernmost side of your house. (Get it? "Western"?) If you don't know which side that is, get a compass and figure it out. (*Hint:* The sun always goes down in the west!)

listen to the music

You use steel to sharpen steel,
*   and one friend sharpens another. (Prov. 27:17)*

So let's do it—full of belief, confident that we're presentable inside and out. Let's keep a firm grip on the promises that keep us going. [God] always keeps his word. Let's see how inventive we can be in encouraging love and helping out, not avoiding worshiping together as some do but spurring each other on, especially as we see the big Day approaching. (Heb. 10:22–24)

what we hear

Spurs probably don't feel so good if you happen to be the horse. They have only one purpose: to get a beast on the move—usually forward. In marriage we're called to be "agitants" for positive change in each other. Yet there's a big difference between being an *agitant* and being an *irritant*. When we're spurring each other on toward change, we see a mutually desired destination—somewhere we both want to be that makes it worth putting on the positive pressure. Conversely, we can "ride" our mates about something to the point of becoming a discouragement to them. This is why Paul says that we should see how "inventive" we can be in our encouragement—actively involved in keeping our spouse moving forward. Some days that might be through a stimulating conversation; sometimes it involves actions that show our support. Notice that our encouragement should include elements of belief (seeing beyond the present state), confidence (knowing that God is in each of us and that his potential through us is limitless), and challenge (throwing out a big goal and dreaming toward it together). Paul also urges us to keep on worshipping together because it keeps us moving in accordance with the only source of lasting change: the power of God in our lives.

what do you hear?

In what ways are you an agitant for change and growth in your mate's life?

What are your spouse's dreams at this point in his or her life?

Ask your mate how you can best spur him or her on—more verbal support or more actions?

extended play

Encourage your love to do something you know he or she is longing to do. Better yet, do it together!

forty nine

A Heart-y Woman

rhythm

Go to the pantry—or wherever you keep the canned goods.

listen to the music

A hearty wife invigorates her husband,
but a frigid woman is cancer in the bones. (Prov. 12:4)

A good woman is hard to find,
and worth far more than diamonds.

Her husband trusts her without reserve,
and never has reason to regret it.

Never spiteful, she treats him generously
all her life long. (Prov. 31:10–12)

what we hear

Hearty just sounds like a word that should be followed by the word *stew*. Meaty. Full of nourishment and sustenance. Bountiful. Generous. Mmm, mmm, good! We can't think of too many women who would want to be characterized as "stewlike," but there's no denying that there's something satisfying about substance. A woman can be beautiful to behold *and* be good in the foxhole. These qualities aren't antithetical. There's nothing wrong with a girlie girl, but these passages in Proverbs remind us that a good woman not only has a warm heart and keeps the invitation open to receive her man, but she also isn't afraid to roll up her sleeves. She's a life giver, not a love scrimper. The term *invigorates* literally means "to impart vigor, strength, or vitality"—to bring more life to her man. In fact, that's a great measurement of a wife's "hearty-ness."

Does your man seem more alive around you, or do you see the life drain out of him in your presence? A good wife holds nothing back from her lover, and he trusts her implicitly because of it. In the immortal words of the MasterCard commercial, a good wife is "priceless."

what do you hear?

Would you characterize your marriage as full of vim, vigor, and vitality? If not, what ingredients do you think are missing?

In what ways are you a generous lover?

Complete this sentence: "I really love it when you _____ _____."

extended play

Now fulfill the filled-in-blank above.

fifty

"Let's Work Our Way Down"

rhythm

Spread a blanket on the floor. Toss in as many throw pillows as you like and jump in.

listen to the music

You're so beautiful, my darling,
    so beautiful, and your dove eyes are veiled

By your hair as it flows and shimmers,
    like a flock of goats in the distance
    streaming down a hillside in the sunshine.

Your smile is generous and full—
    expressive and strong and clean.

Your lips are jewel red,
    your mouth elegant and inviting,
    your veiled cheeks soft and radiant.

The smooth, lithe lines of your neck
    command notice—all heads turn in awe and admiration!

Your breasts are like fawns,
  twins of a gazelle, grazing among the first spring flowers.

The sweet, fragrant curves of your body,
  the soft, spiced contours of your flesh

Invite me, and I come. I stay
  until dawn breathes its light and night slips away.

You're beautiful from head to toe, my dear love,
  beautiful beyond compare, absolutely flawless. (Song 4:1–7)

what we hear

This is one guy who knows where women are turned on—between the ears! Solomon knew how to give a complete compliment that would hit a woman square in her most erogenous zone: her brain. His bedroom talk was unparalleled. What woman wouldn't want to give herself completely to a husband who hasn't just looked at her but has really *seen* her?

American women are the most insecure creatures about their physical attractiveness. In one Internet survey, women rated their insecurities about their bodies as the top reason they avoid sex. It therefore falls to husbands to talk about how pleasing their wives are to them. Most guys think their woman is beautiful in many ways, and they honestly believe that *thinking* it is enough. "Surely she can tell how much she turns me on," they insist. But in the same way that a man says, "I'm not a mind reader; you have to tell me what you need," a woman says,

"Hey, I'm not a mind reader either; tell me what you see in me!" It takes a heap of compliments to counteract the images of airbrushed perfection that bombard your wife daily. She knows what she sees on TV and how she doesn't measure up. She knows how *she* feels about what she sees in the mirror. She needs you to tell her what the view is from *your* eyes.

what do you hear?

Why is it valuable to couple actions with words?

How can you be your lover's "mirror" to offset the images of perfection and the messages of comparison that he or she receives every single day from our culture?

How comfortable are you with giving your mate compliments? How about when you're on the receiving end?

extended play

Get positively Solomonish, men. Start at the top of your lover's body and work your way down, lavishing her with words of praise for her body. She may protest outwardly, but you can bet she'll be getting an inner boost from every complimentary word.

fifty one

"Oooowweeee – You're So Big and Strong"

rhythm

Ladies, stand in front of a mirror, with your man in front.

listen to the music

My dear lover glows with health—
  red-blooded, radiant!

He's one in a million.
  There's no one quite like him!

My golden one, pure and untarnished,
  with raven black curls tumbling across his shoulders.

His eyes are like doves, soft and bright,
  but deep-set, brimming with meaning, like wells of water.

His face is rugged, his beard smells like sage,
  His voice, his words, warm and reassuring.

Fine muscles ripple beneath his skin,
  quiet and beautiful.

His torso is the work of a sculptor,
  hard and smooth as ivory.

He stands tall, like a cedar,
  strong and deep-rooted,

A rugged mountain of a man,
  aromatic with wood and stone.

His words are kisses, his kisses words.
  Everything about him delights me, thrills me through and
  through.

That's my lover, that's my man,
  dear Jerusalem sisters. (Song 5:10–16)

what we hear

Turnabout is fair play. Guys don't really *need* these kinds of compliments to fuel their desire for intimacy. (In fact, we've figured out that there's almost no situation—other than bringing up finances during foreplay—that can prevent a man from feeling physical arousal!) But men enjoy a sincere compliment every once in a while too. Guys love to be admired and appreciated for their, well, *manliness*. Just the fact that his woman notices and tells the girls, "Mmm, that's my man!" can do your husband's psyche a world of good. And notice that the compliments are about his physique, his depth, his size, his words—the total package. In her eyes, he's really got it going on. That's all the fuel a man needs to keep going for another ten thousand miles.

what do you hear?

Define *manly*. (Him first, then her.)

Guys, how often could you take a word of admiration from your woman?

Ladies, can you articulate how your man's manliness contributes to your sense of womanliness?

extended play

What part of your body would you love to have touched more often? Your face? Your neck? Your waist? Other?

fifty two

"I Know You by Part"

rhythm

Plant yourselves anyplace you can view a landscape and make some visual comparisons.

listen to the music

Shapely and graceful your sandaled feet,
  and queenly your movement—

Your limbs are lithe and elegant,
  the work of a master artist.

Your body is a chalice,
  wine-filled.

Your skin is silken and tawny
  like a field of wheat touched by the breeze.

Your breasts are like fawns,
  twins of a gazelle.

Your neck is carved ivory, curved and slender.

Your eyes are wells of light, deep with mystery.
  Quintessentially feminine!

Your profile turns all heads,
*   commanding attention.*

The feelings I get when I see the high mountain ranges
*   —stirrings of desire, longings for the heights—*

Remind me of you,
*   and I'm spoiled for anyone else!*

Your beauty, within and without, is absolute,
*   dear lover, close companion.*

You are tall and supple, like the palm tree,
*   and your full breasts are like sweet clusters of dates.*

I say, "I'm going to climb that palm tree!
*   I'm going to caress its fruit!"*

Oh yes! Your breasts
*   will be clusters of sweet fruit to me,*

Your breath clean and cool like fresh mint,
*   your tongue and lips like the best wine. (Song 7:1–8)*

what we hear

When we were in Italy, we saw a lot of sculptures with a lot of body parts. The sculptors were very intentional about infusing their art with great detail, down to the veins and muscle curves *and everything else*. Tourists can even purchase postcards that feature different body parts from a sculpture (like just a hand or an abdomen), and the work of art can easily be identified by that single element.

The compliments Solomon gives in his song are about both the beauty of his lover's individual parts and the beauty of her character. He is telling her that as much as he appreciates the view, he knows there's an invaluable element about her that is more than skin deep. And his use of simile shows that *everything* he sees reminds him of her. Even when she's not around, he has her body committed to memory in great detail. He translates these thoughts into ideas of physical intimacy. (*Note:* This isn't a stretch for guys. Studies tell us that men think about sex an average of once every fifty-two seconds. OK, that may be a slight exaggeration, but not by much!) Men are visual creatures, and Solomon's lover has obviously given him lots of "visions" that have spoiled him for anyone else. He's a goner and isn't ashamed to say so. Not to mention the "really love your peaches, wanna shake your tree" part. (And you probably thought the Steve Miller Band made that up!)

what do you hear?

What's your favorite visual memory of your mate?

How do you locate your lover in a sea of people?

Tell your lover about something inside of him or her that you consider beautiful.

extended play

Have fun completing this sentence for each other: "My favorite part of your body is _____, and the reason is _____."

fifty three

Your Money or Your Life

rhythm

Drag your past three bank statements out on the table. Study them for five minutes.

listen to the music

Don't wear yourself out trying to get rich;
restrain yourself!

Riches disappear in the blink of an eye;
wealth sprouts wings
and flies off into the wild blue yonder. (Prov. 23:4–5)

You can't worship two gods at once. Loving one god, you'll end up hating the other. Adoration of one feeds contempt for the other. You can't worship God and Money both.

If you decide for God, living a life of God-worship, it follows that you don't fuss about what's on the table at mealtimes or whether the clothes in your closet are in fashion. There is far more to your life than the food you put in your stomach, more to your outer appearance than the clothes you hang on your body. (Matt. 6:24–25)

A devout life does bring wealth, but it's the rich simplicity of being yourself before God. Since we entered the world penniless and will leave it penniless, if we have bread on the table and shoes on our feet, that's enough.

Lust for money brings trouble and nothing but trouble. Going down that path, some lose their footing in the faith completely and live to regret it bitterly ever after. (1 Tim. 6:6–8, 10)

what we hear

The statistic can be hard to believe, but more marriages sink from hitting the iceberg called "financial stress" than almost any other issue. In a twist that only God could arrange, it's typical for a spender to marry a saver, and then they get to spend the rest of their lives figuring out how to accommodate the bent of the other—or not. Many couples just can't take the conflict. For a man, not feeling like a great provider saps his sense of competency, and for a woman, not feeling cared for is tantamount to emotional abandonment. So, in a way, it's not such a stretch to see how money issues factor prominently in marital breakups.

Jesus never advocated that people not have money. His beef was with the amount of time we spend worrying about it—how to get it, how to hoard it, how to spend it, how to get more of it—and the discontent that inevitably follows when "a little more" is never quite enough. If your eyes are on the Joneses, satisfaction is perpetually out of reach. *Got food on the table? Got shoes on your feet? Good to go.* And don't forget, you *are* the Joneses to someone else.

what do you hear?

Discuss the question "How will we know when we have 'enough'?"

You're exchanging your lives for something. What is it?

What money habits, values, and weirdnesses did you learn from your families of origin?

extended play

Establish a "love fund" and put a dollar or a five in it each time you make love. See how quickly you can save enough money for a little vacation!

fifty four

It Comes with the Territory

rhythm

Go to the room that's cleanest because you never use it.

listen to the music

Where there are no oxen, the manger is empty,
  but from the strength of an ox comes an abundant harvest.
  (Prov. 14:4 NIV)

what we hear

We've been married long enough to have a few euphemisms to describe things. For instance, we don't ever say "fight"; we prefer to say "intense fellowship" or "spontaneous conversational-growth opportunity." This proverb would qualify as one of those "Thank you so much, Captain Obvious" statements: If there's no ox in the barn, the barn never gets messed up. There are no ox chips, no ox pooh. You know, the stuff you have to shovel? With the ox come the ox chips. Or to put it more plainly, ox pooh happens. It's part and parcel of the ox package.

If you're in a relationship, you'll reap the rewards (abundant harvest) of relationship (love, friendship, intimacy, history, family), and you'll also have to deal with the other stuff that comes with the territory (disagreements, arguments, misunderstandings, miscommunications; you know, fights!). The trick is to keep the barn clean on a daily basis instead of waiting until you're waist deep in ox pooh. If you want to be happily married, you have to keep short accounts and make sure you do the daily emotional "shoveling." It's a small price to pay for the trade-off of an abundant, productive partnership.

what do you hear?

What is the current state of your marital "barn"? Clean or dirty?

What are your rules of engagement when it comes to disagreements?

What practical steps could you take to help you "fight short, fight fair, and shovel quickly"?

extended play

Shoveling can be fun. Recall the best time you ever had making up from a fight.

fifty five

The Fear Factor

rhythm
Head out to your yard after dark.

listen to the music
God is love. When we take up permanent residence in a life of love, we live in God and God lives in us. This way, love has the run of the house, becomes at home and mature in us, so that we're free of worry on Judgment Day—our standing in the world is identical to Christ's. There is no room in love for fear. Well-formed love banishes fear. Since fear is crippling, a fearful life—fear of death, fear of judgment—is one not yet fully formed in love.

We, though, are going to love—love and be loved. First we were loved, now we love. He loved us first. (1 John 4:17–19)

For God has not given us a spirit of fear, but of power and of love and of a sound mind. (2 Tim. 1:7 NKJV)

what we hear
Yet another piece of knowledge that comes with being married to someone: You know your mate's personal phobias. From spiders to heights to enclosed spaces, we all have our lists of things that make us

shriek, sweat, lose sleep, and have nightmares. When it comes to true intimacy, this spiritual concept tests our inner fears and issues: As our love grows, the fear we have of *truly being known* will be displaced.

Fear is a formidable barrier to intimacy; in fact, intimacy and fear are mutually exclusive. And what exactly are we afraid of? At the root, rejection and the possibility of abandonment. *Will you love me if you really know me? Will you leave me if you really know me?* By contrast, love creates a place where fear has no place. The term *banished* is pretty descriptive, like a king pronouncing that someone can never reenter his kingdom. Perfect love has a no-tolerance policy for fear, and as we let God's love take up more and more space in our lives, fear eventually gets edged out. Remember: No matter how great our capacity for fear, our capacity to love will always be greater.

what do you hear?

What was your biggest fear when you were a child? Does it seem silly to you now? Compare it with your current biggest fear.

What would you do if you had no fear?

What would you say is the ratio of fear to perfect love in your life right now?

extended play

It's good to have someone you trust who knows your fears. Pray together that perfect love will replace fear in your spouse's life.

fifty six

You'll Grow into It

rhythm

Find a playground, complete with swing sets, teeter-totters, and merry-go-rounds.

listen to the music

> But Jesus said, "Not everyone is mature enough to live a married life. It requires a certain aptitude and grace. Marriage isn't for everyone. Some, from birth seemingly, never give marriage a thought. Others never get asked—or accepted. And some decide not to get married for kingdom reasons. But if you're capable of growing into the largeness of marriage, do it." (Matt. 19:11–12)

what we hear

Remember when you were little, and your mom would buy you clothes a size or two too big and say those dreaded words, "Don't worry; you'll grow into it"? It wasn't so much that you were worried that you'd never fill out the clothes, just that it was going to be awkward for a while. Jesus may not have been married himself, but he sure had things to say on the subject! In Matthew he commented on what it takes to have a successful, committed, long-term union: growth and flexibility.

Marriage is a calling of a different kind, a calling to give yourself wholly to a universe you could never inhabit alone. It requires grace, maturity, and the ability to envision creating something larger than the sum of two parts. Sure, each of you will stand before God to give separate accounts of your lives, but the stewardship of this entity called "our marriage" will be on the accounting ledger too. As Jesus said, it isn't for everyone. But by your choice and your commitment, you're in. And no matter how awkward the growth spurts may be, don't worry, you'll both grow into it.

what do you hear?

On a scale of 1 to 10, how ready do you think each of you were to be married at the time you said "I do"?

What about your marriage makes you better together than you are separate?

What has been your biggest growing pain to date?

extended play

Recall your first encounter—each describing in detail the feelings that ran through your head (and other body parts). Also talk about the moment you knew you were ready to grow into the "largeness of marriage."

fifty seven

Drop It Already

rhythm

Come together wherever you keep your suitcases. (You know, the baggage.)

listen to the music

God has given us the task of telling everyone what he is doing. We're Christ's representatives. God uses us to persuade men and women to drop their differences and enter into God's work of making things right between them. We're speaking for Christ himself now: Become friends with God; he's already a friend with you. (2 Cor. 5:18–20)

This is how I want you to conduct yourself in these matters. If you enter your place of worship and, about to make an offering, you suddenly remember a grudge a friend has against you, abandon your offering, leave immediately, go to this friend and make things right. Then and only then, come back and work things out with God. (Matt. 5:23)

what we hear

What do you need to make any horror movie more believable? Just a well-established grudge, of course! It explains everything the scary person does for the next ninety minutes. It's motivational—in a twisted, criminal way. A grudge is easy to come by but hard to shake. Sometimes we can't even remember what started it; we just know this: I'm mad, and therefore, you must be responsible.

How interesting that Paul tells us we're not entitled to hold a grudge. If God, for Christ's sake, could drop his grudge against us, we're really treading into arrogant territory when we think we have the right to hold on to our anger over an offense. It flies in the face of the life of reconciliation God has called us to. In fact, the very core of the good news of Jesus Christ is that the power of forgiveness can overcome anything, and we have the ability, with God's help, to choose to drop an offense. There are several ways to determine if you've truly dropped it. (They all start with Bs so they're easy to remember.)

1. *Blame*—Are you still blaming someone for your current unhappiness? Then forgiveness is still an issue.

2. *Bitterness*—Are you keeping score? Are you looking for evidence that proves your point?

3. *Behavior*—Do you find yourself overreacting to your spouse because something he or she is doing is reminding you of someone else who offended you?

4. *Baggage*—Do you feel as though you're carrying around some sort of heavy emotional weight, but you just can't put your finger on it?

This baggage of unforgiveness can weigh you down and

keep you from enjoying a clear path of communication with God and your spouse. No need to keep dragging it from place to place. Drop it already!

what do you hear?

Do you think you have some unresolved forgiveness issues that are weighing you down? If so, what are they?

How does holding a grudge affect your intimacy with your partner?

Which of the Bs in the previous list is most difficult for you?

extended play

Pray for each other regarding any "unforgiveness baggage." Some of it may have been attached to you so long that it has become almost comfortable. How can you help each other be free from grudges?

fifty eight

Keeping the Peace

rhythm

Head to the most "civilized" space in your house—the room where you allow no horseplay.

listen to the music

Summing up: Be agreeable, be sympathetic, be loving, be compassionate, be humble. That goes for all of you, no exceptions. No retaliation. No sharp-tongued sarcasm. Instead, bless—that's your job, to bless. You'll be a blessing and also get a blessing.

Whoever wants to embrace life
   and see the day fill up with good,

Here's what you do:
   Say nothing evil or hurtful;

Snub evil and cultivate good;
   run after peace for all you're worth. (1 Peter 3:8–11)

what we hear

We have the lyrics from Billy Joel's "Just the Way You Are" circling around in our brains. The concept of loving each other just the way we are is nice, but really, don't we wish our mate would change just a little bit? Not anything that would alter his or her personality, just those annoying habits—especially in those little areas that drive us batty.

The law-enforcement term *disturbing the peace* is a finable offense, but it isn't very well defined. Seems all sorts of behavior can get you arrested under that broad category. We know when we're disturbing our partner's peace. Many of our behaviors not only contradict our mate's preferences but also upset the equilibrium of our home and throw up roadblocks to every sort of intimacy. Why we invite this into our lives is a mystery, but the solution isn't. The apostle Peter summed it up in a single word: "bless." Your one and only job is to bless your spouse. That means every action, every word, every plan needs to be run through this filter: "Will this bless him or her?"

What kind of personal utopia could this kind of thinking usher into our marriages if it became our modus operandi? Wouldn't it be fun to find out?

what do you hear?

Name one thing your mate did recently that really blessed you.

Would you describe your household as "full of peace?" Why or why not?

Name one thing you do that disturbs the peace with your spouse. What steps can you take to do it less often?

extended play

What do you think is the legacy of your marriage? How will it be remembered?

fifty nine

Sacred Bodies

rhythm

Look at your wedding pictures.

listen to the music

There's more to sex than mere skin on skin. Sex is as much spiritual mystery as physical fact. As written in Scripture, "The two become one." Since we want to become spiritually one with the Master, we must not pursue the kind of sex that avoids commitment and intimacy, leaving us more lonely than ever—the kind of sex that can never "become one." There is a sense in which sexual sins are different from all others. In sexual sin we violate the sacredness of our own bodies, these bodies that were made for God-given and God-modeled love, for "becoming one" with another. Or didn't you realize that your body is a sacred place, the place of the Holy Spirit? (1 Cor. 6:16–19)

what we hear

We've said elsewhere in this book that we belong to each other. And that's right. But we also belong to someone else, someone who paid the ultimate price to have the right to direct our lives.

We belong first and foremost to God. He has a desire for us to be in union with him, and out of that, to have sex that encourages "oneness" with our mate, not just self-gratification. It's possible to have sex without intimacy. But this isn't the kind of sex God desires for his people. As Paul wrote, it's more than "skin on skin." It's not just primal; it's spiritual. There's an element to our sexuality in which we recognize that God gave us this gift of physical pleasure to bring us closer to each other and to him. In the old Quaker vows of marriage, one of the statements the couple repeats is "Thee I worship with my body." In truth, our physical intimacy is a spiritual mystery, and when we recognize what a gift from the hand of God it is, it becomes a form of worship.

what do you hear?

In what ways does physical intimacy with your mate strike you as spiritual?

When you were becoming an adult, was this concept ever instilled to you, or is it a new concept that you have to plant into your own life together?

Talk about your favorite memory from your wedding day (or night).

extended play

Pray together and ask God to help you be more aware of his presence in your intimate moments.

sixty

Made for Each Other

rhythm

Go to the kitchen and spread peanut butter on one piece of bread and jelly on the other. Let the slices lie there separately while you read on.

listen to the music

Haven't you read in your Bible that the Creator originally made man and woman for each other, male and female? And because of this, a man leaves father and mother and is firmly bonded to his wife, becoming one flesh—no longer two bodies but one. Because God created this organic union of the two sexes, no one should desecrate his art by cutting them apart. (Matt. 19:4)

what we hear

Some things just don't make sense apart—peanut butter without jelly, New York without Broadway, Sonny without Cher. Some things just *need* to be together and are elevated to art status when combined. God's design for a man and a woman together was that these two entities fit perfectly (like puzzle pieces), and when they do, their union would be a wonder and beauty to behold. Matthew tells us that God's design for "this organic union" was his highest form of art, and he doesn't like anything that messes with his art.

We aren't suggesting that either person in the marriage relationship couldn't exist on his or her own, but the union is richer somehow than its individual parts. We truly begin to value our marriage when we see the divine art that occurs as our minds, bodies, and spirits are mingled together in this organic union. The term *organic* denotes "living, changing, of natural origin." Who among us would say that nothing has changed since the day we said "I do"? Our marriages grow and change over time, and the work of art only appreciates in value. Can you say that although it's possible that you could exist without each other, life just wouldn't make as much sense? The next time you go out together (or stay in, for that matter!), remember that together you are gallery worthy.

what do you hear?

If your love were depicted in a gallery, would it be a painting or a sculpture? Why?

In Matthew 19, Jesus was explaining why divorce is such an affront to God. What are your views on divorce?

What is it about your union that makes it inconceivable that you could be apart?

extended play

Find a piece of art for your home that depicts and celebrates your love as a couple. (Oh, right, we almost forgot. Put the peanut butter and jelly together and eat your sandwich already!)

encore

If God grants you both length of years, you have a very good chance of being married longer than you were single, longer than you fill an active parenting role (if you have children), and even longer than you have a career. So your marriage is worthy of your time and attention. This relationship that you have vowed to nurture, honor, and protect is your gift to each other and your love legacy to the world.

"One final word, friends," Paul wrote. *"We ask you—urge is more like it—that you keep on doing what we told you to do to please God, not in a dogged religious plod, but in a living, spirited dance. You know the guidelines we laid out for you from the Master Jesus. God wants you to live a pure life." (1 Thess. 4:1–2)*

Though this sounds like a monumental undertaking, we're called to "dance" the spirited dance with liveliness, joy, holiness, anticipation, and true intimacy of every kind. And not just dance for dancing's sake, but because that joyous, spirited kind of dance infuses us with enthusiasm to follow God and embrace his precepts for living, which ultimately results in the by-product of purity. And purity is the ultimate antidote for the very thing that would keep us separated and avoiding intimacy: shame.

If you could see us right now, you'd see that we're giving you a standing ovation. Congratulations on finding the back of the book. We hope you're here because you've gotten through most (if not all) of the devotions, and your marriage is stronger than it was before you started because you've read and talked and played and prayed together.

But the song isn't over! We pray that these pages have given you a template of sorts for a never-ending coming together of a man and a woman before God, opening his Word and giving more freely of yourselves because you've been changed by the power of his message. Consider it your personal encore of a song we may have helped you rediscover. You can create ongoing encounters of your own because God's Word is a living source of never-ending inspiration.

It's our prayer that your marriage will become more intimate each day as you live and learn about each other and your Creator. We know that every time you come together with the intent of growing in true intimacy—physical, emotional, and spiritual— you're taking another step toward fulfilling the purpose God had in mind when he brought you together. When that happens, you'll find that your three-corded strand is unbreakable. May his love keep your love.

And in the words of that Shakespeare dude, "If music be the food of love, play on."